SOLO PRESS

Carpinteria, California and North Wilkesboro, North Carolina

Solo Number 4

Publisher/Editor:	Glenna Luschei
Editors:	David Oliveira Jackson Wheeler
Review Editor:	Kevin Clark
Assistant Editors:	Valentina Gnup Bruce Schmidt
Contributing Editors:	Wendy Lawton Dorothy Owen
Production & Design:	Laura Davison
Circulation:	Dana F. Yudovin Deborah Gran

Solo is an independent journal of poetry published annually by Solo Press.

For subscribers of *Café Solo*, this issue serves as series 32, 33 and 34.

Address all correspondence to the editorial offices located at: 5146 Foothill Road, Carpinteria, California 93013; or 508 Finley Street, North Wilkesboro, North Carolina 28659.

Individual subscription (two issues): $18; Foreign: $30.

Café Solo is listed in the American Humanities Index, provided by Whitston Publishing Co., PO Box 958, Troy, NY 12181.

Publisher's Foreword

Athens of the West! That's what they called Iowa City in the fifties when I first met Donald Justice, cover artist and poet. This Iowa was far different from the Loess Hills Valley where I grew up detasseling corn in the blaze of summer. We froze in cold-morning pickup trucks but stripped to swimming suits in the sweltering afternoon, never too tired to go roller skating at night. This was the Iowa of illustrious poets and writers. I sat in a classroom with Robert Frost whose profile looked like one of the presidents on Mt. Rushmore. It was still freezing though; ice formed inside the walls of our barracks.

I was twenty three, straddling motherhood and struggling to make my own mark as a poet. Paul Engle, workshop founder, told me my poems evoked Robert Penn Warren. How could I, who lived in a barracks and spent her non-poetry hours hanging up diapers to dry in the hallway near the space heater, be compared to the Oxfordian, distinguished Yale professor and Pulitzer Prize-Winner? He explored themes of identity in historical events; I grappled with two babies without washer or dryer. I built a nursery for my Erich, born in the University's Medical Hospital and delivered by students, from our only closet, while trying to hold my own in an unwelcoming city-state. I felt disoriented and alone.

Things got better. We participants were invited to meet other writers at the home of Donald Justice, subsequently my teacher and hero. His Athens gathered together the Esquire Symposium where baseball novelist Mark Harris (*Bang the Drum Slowly*) squared off against Normal Mailer.

Spring brought more gatherings and picnics. Filipino novelist Ben Santos and his wife Aquing invited us over for pancid. I met Robert Mezey and the young family of Richard Power, the Irish novelist and that of Walter Tevis who had just published *The Hustler*. I made friends with two Southern women, Millie and Nancy. People still didn't like my poems but I was happy!

Donald Justice began my journey and that of Solo Press. One of my first memories of him is on a baseball field. With Solo's premiere cover of poets in baseball caps painted by David Oliveira, it seems life has come full cycle. Hang in there despondent members of workshops, you'll find your Justice. As you join the ranking Senate membership of poets, may we open wide the doors to the chamber.

Glenna Luschei
September 24, 2000

III

Table of Contents

Poetry

VI

Reviews

Editors' Note

One of the advantages of being editors is the opportunity to have an ongoing dialogue about poetry and what it is, exactly, that draws one to prefer one form or expression of poetry over another. Clearly we are concerned about the printed poem, and what it conveys from the page. This immediately excludes a popular body of work which exists at poetry slams and performance events—some of it entertaining to watch and hear, most of it failing to some degree when written out on the page. So we acknowledge already a bias toward poems which work on the page, the gift to the reader, as well as those poems which, by virtue of their language are lovely to hear as well, the gift to the listener. And because we are both readers and listeners, we enjoy a good story, the narrative aspect of poetry.

In our fourth issue, we bring you consummate storytellers. Poets like Mark Jarman who wraps his stories in the folds of the sonnet form; the brilliant gems from Ted Kooser, much like hearing family history, piecemeal. Other masters, Patricia Goedicke, Adrian C. Louis, Holly Prado, and Dorothy Barresi, reveal, unerringly with attention to language, form, and that almost indefinable, "poetic voice" stories which pulse through all of us, connecting us to the great human story.

All of these poems touched or moved us in some way, and they become our gift to the world, in print, like one of the labeled objects in Alice in Wonderland; this one says, "Read Me." And if you do, you will be doubly blessed to discover that some poets, like Majorie Agosín will not only sing to you, but will sing in two languages.

David Oliveira
Jackson Wheeler

Dedication

In Memory of
Harry Duncan
and
Ben Santos

and

For friends from the Iowa City Workshop days

and

In Honor of Nancy Duncan, Steve and Millie Berg
John and Ellen Kuiper and Jean Lloyd-Jones

English translations by Celeste Kostopulos-Cooperman

Pisagua

Aquel mudo y hablado desierto
guardó sus cuerpos:
cabezas decapitadas,
manos arqueadas por una soga gris.
El desierto preservó sus vidas.
Por muchos años fue como la nieve eterna,
cuidadosa de lo que se oculta
bajo la tierra.
En la hipnótica aridez,
los muertos aún vivían
para contarte la historia.

Pisagua

That silent yet well-known desert
protected their bodies:
decapitated heads,
hands curved by a gray rope.
The desert preserved their lives.
For many years it was like the eternal snow,
caring for what hides
deep inside the earth.
In the hypnotic dryness,
the dead still lived on
to tell you the story.

Gobi

I

Era hablada la noche del desierto.
A lo lejos el silencio
imaginaba y cantaba.
Hablada era la noche de Gobi,
y el humo de la bruma era
un collar de huellas sobre la arena virgen.

II

A lo lejos alguien rezaba.
Alguien contaba historias.
¿o era la sombra de la muerte
piadosa entre las dunas?

Gobi

I

The desert night spoke.
In the distance the silence
imagined and sang.
The Gobi night spoke
and the steam from the mist was
a necklace of bones over virgin sand.

II

In the distance someone prayed.
Someone told stories.
Or was it the shadow of a merciful
death among the dunes?

Donde anidan los pájaros

En aquel desierto
donde anidaban los pájaros
él conoció mi rostro.
Su mano se inclinaba sobre
la luz como una cruz
de santos de campo extraviado.
Habló de ángeles y amores,
de vientos y gorriones
para que no haya más ira,
para que no haya más
olvido.

Oyó esa voz delgada y aguda,
una voz semejante al origen
de todos los comienzos
y esa voz le dijo:
regresa al desierto
a tejer y destejer las arenas.

Where Birds Nest

In that desert
where birds nested
he became acquainted with my face.
His hand leaned on
the light like a sacred
cross in a lost field.
He spoke of angels and loves,
of wind and sparrows
so that there would be no more rage
no more
oblivion.

He heard that delicate and sharp voice,
a voice resembling the origin
of all beginnings
and that voice told him:
return to the desert
to weave and unweave the grains of sand.

Capsule

So that sleep will be deep and unbroken
        so that morning will be bereft of one more
staggering sorrow so that the body resides,
        at least, within the spongy cage of the skin.
No better than that. No less: sleep enclosed
        behind the eye's closed door, yes any dream
in a tin sleep-bucket and the dog rattling
        like a stone. Yes, night
        like a fire and no bells.

Heart as Metaphor

The hand, the head, the harrow,
All the turning back we can offer.
Here is the tick of it: nothing sings.
The bell has no sway. The hands
of the heart stop.
                    The poem is an inlet,
a bird. A drum. My end-stopped heart.

Dinner in Miami

Appetizer

"We may live without friends, we may live without books,
but civilized men cannot live without cooks!"

—*Lucille*, by Edward Robert Bulwer, Earl of Lytton

Entrée

The worn-out man and his red-eyed wife
had driven up from the Keys at the end of an awful day
spent wrangling with a son bankrupt once again.
Maybe it might have perked them up
had they known the chef once cooked for Princess Grace.
Maybe not. "You are what you eat. Eat what you are,"
the man declared, downing his stiff drink to order
the bourbon-soaked rib eye with orange chimmichurri.
His wife sighed and could not decide
between the Key West yellowtail
and the cassoulet with confit of duck.

Their lives improved with the appetizers,
the truffled sauce, the capers in the conch piccata,
with the ample portions on oversized plates,
the good wine, the sweet light in the clear glass lamp,
all reminding them of better times, of Paris,
of restaurants on the Boulevard St. Michel,
the Luxembourg Gardens, the moon on the Seine,
the honeymoon that continued on to Malaga.
"Remember that gypsy singer at El Figon?" he asked,
both of them now looking at the list of desserts,
"the one who called himself El Chocoláte?"
She smiled a wide Princess Grace of a smile.
And he, although not given to public displays,
took her hand and kissed it.

Dessert
Chocolate Crunch Bar
with vanilla anglaise, strawberry sauce
and chocolate cigarette

Chocolate. <*chocolatl*, from the Mayan *xocoatl.*
The Aztec royal drink chilled with mountain snow
frothed and spiced with honey and with clove.
Montezuma drank it before going to his wives.
Cortez shipped it home in 1528. Now the couple
shares a plate, while sipping at their sherry,
remembering the song El Chocoláte sang:

> "When will the day come,
> that blissful morning when
> chocolate will be brought to us
> side by side in bed?"

Both of them now grateful, near the end of day,
for dinners that offer ease like poetry or song.

Eddie

Hadn't seen Eddie for some time,
wheeling his chair through traffic,
skinny legs in shorts, t-shirted,
down at the corner off Dixie Highway,
lifting his Coke cup to the drivers
backed up, bumper to bumper, at the light.
Sometimes he slept on the concrete bench
up from Joe's News. Sometimes police
would take him in and he said he didn't mind
because he got three squares and sometimes
a doctor would look at his legs, paralyzed,
he said, since the cop in New York shot him
when he tried to steal a car. Sad story,
of the kind we've learned to live with.

One rainy day he looked so bad, legs
ballooned, ankles to calves, clothes soaked,
I shoved a $20 in his cup. But, like I said,
I hadn't seen him around so yesterday
I stopped and asked this other panhandler
where's Eddie? "Dead," he said. Slammed
by a truck that ran the light, crushed
into his wheelchair. Dead, months ago.

My wife says he's better off dead
but I don't know. Behind his smudged glasses
his eyes were clever. He had a goofy smile
but his patter was sharp. His legs were a mess
and he had to be lonely. But spending days
in the bright fanfare of traffic and
those nights on his bench, with the moon
huge in the palm trees, the highway quiet,
some good dreams must have come to him.

The Spiritual Life, Evening Commute

What if, instead of traveling through God,
towards God,
and His heavenly pajama party
of wings and chandeliers and fat-cheeked *putti*,
puffing our lights and our last breath out of us, upward,
like another song of air in praise,

what if instead of all that
I am driving southbound from Cleveland, Ohio,
my window cracked open
against the small fog my humming makes.
It's raining—what else is new?

Refinery towers walk backwards to the river,
single-file,
holding no one's hand.
As a girl I counted the tops of them as hatted,
brick-jawed cowboys
riding herd to the brilliant orange flames of Sohio:
thirty-six to Akron, forty, Chargrin Falls.
Now Terminal Tower outshines all distances
with its bistros and swanky shops,

its jewels rise white
above the stanchions dripping
pickling acid and steam,
and these words, *liberty, truth, valor,*
on the blackened broad side of LTV Steel as I pass.

I read the words or don't.
It depends on traffic.
Road conditions, which could be fatal,
keep my hand on the sliding, proving wheel.

But what if St. John of the Cross was right?
What if Sister Cletus

in the extremity of her love and our sixth-grade fear
was right, and one short line of sinners
snakes and is received into the longer line
because we *are* sinners, are not God,
and nothing more?

On ramps. Men at Slow Work.
For perilous passage a Honda bears down;
she passes me on the right.
Embarrassing, the nights I've numbed-out and missed my exit.
I've turned for hours in the scorched city neighborhoods,
trying to get home.
And what if we go our entire lives
having never once
been valorous. What then?

                    *

The ones who work the evening shift are coming on.
Kingdom of memory, Mother Steel.
In ancient blue coveralls under huge green windows tilted open
to catch the filthy air, they look
tiny from this distance,

bendable as the action/adventure dolls I bought
my sister's stepson
a hundred Christmases ago. You know the ones:
Masters of the Universe.
Creatures so angry I had to pay $29.95
for the complete set, including Forest of the Doomed
and Moss Man, who emitted a piney
smell when frightened or pressed
hard in the chest. Christ!

I kept losing myself in that crush of iron-jawed mall shoppers.
Those geniuses of direction and velocity
had me spinning

until I sat with my head between my knees
then drank the Diet Coke a giggling shopgirl offered
while pretending to ignore the acned stockboy who was singing—
I remember this—

shock the monkey, shock the monkey,

over and over
into her ear.

     *

So I remind myself,
there are dangers in the suburbs, too.
Distraction, for one. Soft duty for another.
And all the blind soul-shuffling
between the world where my parents roar like trees caught
in the sway of one more
giant snow off Lake Erie,

give us grandchildren, more love,

and the other one, where my students dangle
untied purple tennis shoes
over desktops,
and twist their ponytails endlessly,
and offer up their heart-shaped trusts in loopy handwriting
with daisies
to dot the *i*'s:

"Hamlet is Hamlet because he takes his own sweet time."

     *

So do I.
On the radio, Chippie Hill or Bird,
the Replacements singing, "all over but the shouting."
I'm not lost, but the rain
taps its fingers on the sideview mirror,
the metronome of wiper blades
ticking one thought in my brain:

maybe this is not the world.
Maybe this is the world as we pass it
no matter how many questions we ask, or of Whom.

In Brecksville and Hudson and Shaker Heights, I've imagined lives
more real than my own,
the rooted ones.
A woman dimming the light above her dinner table
to the tremolo of teakettle,
her husband rattling the *Plain Dealer* in the next room, Sports & Obits.
My students in bars,
drinking to running backs and joy.

And me, still here idling,
not unhappy,
though purpose or certainty of thought
seem as far away as my exit,
or the next new world caught between a half-gone
Chrysler and this Galaxy
I'm signalling to—

hurry up, little man. Hurry up.

On Hearing of Your Fourth Marriage, a Judgmental Poem, Meanly Meant

> *"An advisory has been issued for the westbound*
> *Ventura Freeway, where a mattress has fallen*
> *into the number four lane."*

To see a mattress fly!
It lets go of rings of resistance.
It is a flightless bird
devolving to the freeway's best lane.

The sudden self
grants this permission, slip-knotted:
marriage, divorce, marriage, divorce, marriage, divorce
(and divorce again?)

with wobble, flip, ass over teakettle,
who knows what will happen next
when calamity
slides from the bed of the long pickup in front of you.

Carelessly tied?
Of course. Now it zing, zang, zungs
orange cones and whipped commuters
screeching left of center to miss it.

Then to see it walk a moment on hind legs.
A mattress like a monster.
A monster like a newborn man
falling flat on his face, and you,

distracted by your own astonishing life in romance,
aim straight for it, and why not
grind sawdust from floral brocade?
Springs up-coil like

rawest shoots of April.
Was it once a conjugal nest? Highly irrelevant.
Survival calls for damage first,
followed by change; though aging,

your reflexes are legendary.
Who needs road or gravity or direction?
Your wheels spin the way
mice run heedless their cold wheel

at midnight.
The way karma and the Kama Sutra
keep turning you into yourself, over and over,
with others.

Bad at love,
does love at your age feel
exactly like driving
on the back of an extra-firm magic carpet?

You're getting everywhere and nowhere,
suspended again
between hope and terror,
between death and really terrific support.

Second Freeing from Sylla

Hired lodgings
at a low rate

All purity & uprightness
gone

I lived under the
same roof with him

I upstairs, he down
at a little higher rent

Oh yes, we knew each other
we knew, indeed.

Now, Blotchface in power
says I must die

(What hate now from
his blue eyes).

And vanity the only
why—lest I tell all.

Now I'm due to be
—smashed from the high rock.

Yet, yet what a lover—
eh, old Nicopolis?
eh, young Metrobius?

Phaeton
for Maxine Kumin

He sees the light cart in the paddock,
isn't thinking of the time he spooked a month ago—
the cart half-hitched, the gate unlocked—
and you held on. Today he's calm,

standing quietly as you thread the traces through the
footman's loop and ask him to back up. I stand
by his Arab head, masked in mosquito netting, and then
join you in the seat that substitutes, today, for his back.

Easy in your hands, he trots up the road, ears alert
to your voice, the encouraging praise, the clucks that urge him
past laziness when the hill steepens. Your hands know
the give and take of the canter, the sweet compromise

that adjudicates his power and your will. In our helmets,
under these summer trees, we are as safe as we will ever be.

Sonnet in Summer

How eager are the lovers to leave the crowd,
      wander away from the small display of fireworks,
smoke rising over the building, loud
      groups of three or four with drinks in paper cups.
They are happy to sit on the balcony and share a cigarette
      in the dark, and talk, knowing
that talk is the soul's way of laying down a blanket
      for the body. Because they know that nothing
lasts, they name the summer scenes—
      cows in a field, crows in the trees——and offer
little stories of the past, fleshing
      out mother and father, brother and sister.
Soon they begin the ordinary journey over each
      other's bodies: sand dune, bay, ocean, beach.

Mail Bomb

A coiled spring more delicate
than a child's finger, the metal
only bending one way or it will break,
and time too, moving only one way,
measured by grains falling, the tick
of a watch, the slow decay of atoms.
I am too large to understand
how quickly we are unwrapped,
the small things we are
exploded. Someone is dead,
and it's not even me.

It seems like me, my body
stunned so I realize only later
the package filled the room,
its small world of eye
becoming monstrously large,
its patient waiting for acceptance
blowing outward.
Someone will come to piece us together.
Someone will find our truth.
This is what survivors think
as they examine their hands.

The lines on their palms
appear intact, the fine hair
of their forearms unsinged,
until they see in the shattered
mirror the hundred loving faces
of as many rooms.

The Well

As in the old country, they dug them
wide enough to climb into.

But the man with pick and shovel,
who took the ground from under himself,

was not there, where I helped my mother
pull off the boards that saved from falling in

dogs, children, the nightroaming
drunks. We stared down

to the cast of light upon the trash
that grew a scurry of rats

where once the digger stood.
He must have lowered himself,

foot, then knee, then waist.
Grass at his eyes, he went under

until the sky receded
to a circle of blue.

Heaven no more
than the span of thumb wrapped

to forefinger, a little 0.
Then, the water seeping in.

How did he get out? I asked her.
My mother, imagining no more

than what we saw, tossed in
the day's trash, and said, *Who?*

I don't know, I said.
In Brookside, the wells went bad

house by house. Their stones were pulled down,
their bottoms filled. Except the one

old man Chervinsky kept, neat with flowers
around its sides. The roof of cedar singles

held straight. The bucket was ready
for the pulley's creak and swing.

He showed me how the well
stayed cool on blazing days.

He turned the wooden crank
and tipped the water toward me,

undrinkable mirror reflecting the sky
and my fingers dipping in.

Mr. Bloom's Party

Old Harold Bloom, posting along the front
of Barnes and Noble's coffee bar, toward shelves
where reams of literary theory culled
the freshly spun out deconstructed selves
of dead white western poets, pulled up short.
The stalls were bare with not a clerk around;
he wandered on to where the poets slept,
and scoffed, since none but he could hear the sound:

"The soul consists of language, as we know,
and word-sounds vanish down time's quiet stream.
Why then do poets try to shape and save,
these odd ephemera which only seem?
I have been one to make this point before."
Before? The very word was like a bell
to toll him back to something not himself,
and stung him with an old familiar smell

of books like bread he once had tried to eat
inside his crib when, thinking far ahead,
his mother substituted books for toys,
and raised a son who never spoke, but read.

Imprint, May 1970

I.

I tell you the skin alone cannot contain
the brawl of a generation—
We burned flags before the helmets
and the dogs rabid with our parents' teeth
locked arms, swaying
and cheered when the match struck
We watched, swore the jelly of napalm
would not silence the corpses
pulled from rice paddies in another world

We thought our skin could still contain
the body blows, the clubs and guns
that struck down one
by one by one by one

2.

I shuffled through white china rows
of lunchtime professors
my black armband for the dead
the frat boys on scholarship
carrying thick-skinned pudding
trays of coffee and cream
counted the days until graduation
Mao and a map of Canada
hidden in their back pockets

3.

A girl on the television in the foyer
bent down, transfixed, screaming
skin stretched taut to the corners
her arms outstretched, protesting
the body of the sprawled boy before her
blood seeps from sinew to dermis
her young face twists
when the camera clicks like a bullet
in a chamber of the heart and we are naive
as though fists had never bruised us before

I stopped dropped
the sheets of colored paper
like blood flowering
on the four-cornered floor

4.

They say even Nixon broke
when they started killing the students
the rupture of skin splitting open
a wound he could not stitch together
so when they told me it was over
I didn't believe them
that scar on membrane and flesh
smoothing over but will not slough off

Gray
for Andrew Engborg, 1989–1995

When it looks as though the day will finally be
sunny, I mourn a little for the clouds
that didn't come, or the squall,

and when the daffodils rise
open-faced one morning in March
in an orderly row,

some small stone sinks in the pool of me
and the ripples along the surface signal
a letting go I didn't want.

Though I moved on purpose to this place
where summer lingers by inching
like a stain into autumn and spring, where winter

rattles only briefly in white-face,
some human truth
streaking through the grease paint,

these days it's only haze I love,
unnameable weather,
an uneventful sky that resembles despair but isn't,

its grayness insisting gray is all there is,
a smudged newsprint that erases the news,
a calming absence which removes for awhile

the absence of you, child, and the accident that left
just your mother alive. She strapped you snug in your car seat
and kissed your head, and then the sun grew brilliant

and wild on the highway's edge.

Today

If you called, I'd answer.
I'd try to find a voice

to touch your face,
until we recalled

ourselves—that skin
and hurt—remembering

how kisses
became questions.

I watched you once
from your bed

brushing your dark hair
out before the mirror.

What's beautiful needs
tending, I know.

I have grown flowers
I could not send you.

Eve

kept to herself on the seventh day,
had everywhere
waiting to walk through,
so many new
names to see,
she could have spent all
of paradise looking,
just looking.

She leaned close to sproutings
and openings, cupping her palms
like a mouth around each
bud and setting-on fruit,

raising every first thing to her tongue,
licking the sound of it,
trailing her fingers in water
or sand while she memorized
how each word throbbed
as she uttered it,
standing a little ways off
to the side of the story.
Not wanting to be overheard.

(Shhh.
She's touching her lips
even now as she's
practicing, her fingers
smelling of spittle
and rose petals.)

Cup

What I want to say is the cracked porcelain cup stained with tea.
It's a woman with a soft brogue who pours,
her flushed arm fat and steady. Now you must strain
off the liquid, swish the wash in the cup three times,
turn it over, her mind radiant with geometry.
What I want to say is in leaf at the base and north end of that cup,
known to her, shapes that speak of trysts and leavings,
journeys and robberies, rain-stippled puddles whisked dry by wind
before we were born and yet to change this world.
What I want to tell you is right there in the dregs
spun just so in that room of many odors. You notice
her ridged nails, her pin-curls tinted auburn, her forward poise
at the edge of the hard chair, her bunion-stretched shoes. It's there,
what you came for, promised in the damp leaves meant for you.

for sarah

as the sons of noah watch the sky
so i watch for the white worlds
nightmare   i have been
mistaken for it many times
often i send my shadow through
before i enter a room   if she
does not return i may be safe
sometimes i walk in to find her
circled in kindness   sometimes
the kindness is wearing stormy gloves
this poem is for you sarah
you know what i mean   you wait with us
by the door   a rainbow of us   some
born to the blood and some like you
who have earned it   we watch
holding each other close
preparing for possible rain

how did we understand
before the image of the tree
became the tree

before memory entered our eyes
and lived there while our bodies
began to wither, forgetting.

forty years and i look at you,
lady, but it is not you
it is only a photograph of us

leaning together by our porch
on purdy street, your fingers
posed as if in blessing

me looking down as if blessed.
the image of the tree
is not the tree. i strain

to remember the ease
of your lifting from my scalp,
the feeling   the reality

so i can pass it to my
daughters — "this
is our front yard tree,

it would burn my knees
when i climbed it and
this is my mama,

she is blessing me, braiding
my hair."

Salmon Eater

Where on the spectrum
will be this flesh; how readily
dividing from its bones.
Swallowed, what radiance

small in the bloodstream
jack-knifing against the current
to the still pool where it comes from.

Three wishes are granted. First, how it feels
to turn and go back towards something,
fish tails beating in your temples.
Second, knowing what to do
when you reach that particular

cusp, where heavy weight
has made a place of depth
near the source. And last,
believing what comes through
undistinguished spawn:

sometimes silver-scaled brilliance,
a thing so loved it is done
over and over, not needing a place
to rest or rest itself, only the doing.

Late

I couldn't get the boot laced. The hole
was broken, the lace too short.

And we were out of paper, so we couldn't
revise the text, though our lives had changed.

Also a torn skirt, a broken watch. More
things than I could carry in my suitcase.

Then someone's child, her new skin
a clean page. Someone's replacement,

I thought, but just for a moment—
I had to finish the boot, and I couldn't

take it with me: it belonged in a place
I had to get out of soon. It was late.

Waiting for the Jackson Flyer

Midnight ticks away
on time
station to station around the clock.

Sleepwalkers
scattered along the benches
rest beneath their burdens

the last light gone out
in the New Central Hotel across the street
rows of black windows
now dark as heaven's caves.

Phone poles along the tracks
march off into the night
only their shadows for coats

the moon
rusting in its socket

and we who inherit the earth—
this snow will yet cover us
with its little hieroglyphic
tokens of the life to come.

Elders

My father remembers
fire: blown sparks
from his Uncle Buell's smithing iron
scorching red
eyes in the lilac leaves;
transparent scarves of yellow flame
smoking up from the locust boles
into a lowering February
sky—he and his father

burning off a new tobacco bed;
he and his grandfather
hunting
camped on a bluff above the Cumberland
the two of them
sitting under scattershot stars
his grandfather telling him
of seeing, as a boy,

the *City of Clifton*
blow its boiler
off the Newboro landing,
my father
dreaming that night
of hearing the stricken
cries of the perishing,
of seeing that fire
out on the water. . . .

My father remembers
a needlepoint picture:
Jesus seated in Glory
with the words,

Christ is the Head
    of This House
The Unseen Guest
    at Every Meal
The Silent Listener
    to Every Conversation

that hung above his father's
kitchen chair,
who'd lean back after Sunday dinner
and sing out,

"Well, I'm most done traveling
this rough rocky road
and it's time my soul headed home"
— a game he had with the kids,

who'd sing out,
"Papa
what will you do
if you can't afford the hearse?"

"Sit on my bed
and wait for angels to come."

"What will you do
if you can't afford the preacher?"

"Pay him with quarters
I stole from the moon."

"Papa, what will you do
if you can't afford the casket?"

"Charge it to the wind," he'd sing,
"let the dust settle it. . . ."

My father remembers lying awake
listening to the locusts in the orchard

chirring to split their skins
listening for the screech owl

haunting the cedars' attic rooms
and finally the Jackson Flyer

blue traveler
taking the high curve out of Orton Station

unwinding her long black veil across the Barrens
moaning it out by midnight—

once for those she takes away
twice for those she's leaving.

The Divorce

It was a failure, perhaps,
of imagination. Mine that clung
without remorse or pity to the vicious
words, the bruised shoulder, the kick
down the steps, the wood door gashed
by the airborne wrench. Or the car
in the vector of its rainy skid.
On the rainy road, that afternoon
in winter, a Sunday so long ago. Yes,
it was the car, really, more than anything
else: stalled, atilt, in the muddy
ditch, still in third, the rear view
reflecting him stomping away, angry
all over, furious in his body, hysterical
even in his thinning hair.
He was betting I'd fetch him
as I had in the past, bleating
in terror, pleading he'd stay.

A brief series of dull-toned beeps
informed me the key was still lodged
in ignition. Swiping clear
a temporary arc to peer beneath,
the wipers revealed the empty road
that led to town, the steel-fenced
pastures on either side, the animals miserable
in the icy rain.
               At last look back.
Weather thickening the distance
between us. I couldn't imagine
anything ever it was possible
to change. There was his same old
overcoat, the cheap cloth shoes. And there, too,

was I the same as ever, weak and afraid,
slumped in the corner of a car my beloved
had tried to wreck. God, I was weary.
How simple to slide in the driver's seat,
to turn the key and roar away—
up and out of the ditch forever.

The Poor Bastard

The perpetual hole

      *

the vacated void

      *

the exquisite spoilage
    of a single
        act

      *

the one bad bud that destroyed us all

      *

our circles broken, our spirals
       torn, our centers
deconstructed

      *

Poor bastard, we say
Rotter, we think

      *

surfacing heavily, his body

          gray gun in his hand

            red hole in his head

His Company Thrown Open to the Public

1.
One who hopes our shit don't stink prays in a pew.
Its hard back hurts his back.

His dead boyfriend's dry come glitters
on the comforter he presses to his cheek.

2.
He bows his head
as if his flesh
were a teardrop, surrender

welling though his nervous system's
web of feeling our fingers could tickle,
pop, pointing

out a consciousness
which is contentless,
conscienceless,

a blaze of abstraction he actually saw
once, sunset hitting a rearview mirror,
an explosion in a desert.

His eyes, each one the weight
of a collapsing star, withdrew
to hide among his privates.

3.
If he were infected, would he stare
into our singing faces
or hide his eyes behind his hand,
seeing no evil, no good?

Would he squat
under an exit sign
and listen to our singing,
happy to be breathing?

He might feel sort of pointlessly humane,
forgiving every body who hurt him,
our smiles shining not far away
from his flinching face.

The Blade

I thought I saw what an angel of death might be
at the Mission San Juan Bautista.
She bent above cased relics in the gift shop.
She wore the habit of a Franciscan nun.
Her face framed by a brown veil was white
as paper. She lingered near the rosaries.
She wouldn't look up or smile even though
I stared too long. Her features carved from ivory
suppressed an anger held at her center
like an invisible sabre of light.
In the mortification of her flesh
by the denial of all worldly pleasure
she thought she'd be a pure intelligence.
But the body's separation from the mind,
or soul, whatever it may be, creates
an innocence so terrible it runs
its blade among the roots of things alive
severing some from what we once called being.
I stuffed some bills in the collection box
so I might have good luck when I emerged
into the sunlight blinking, into a courtyard
of roses, grape arbors, oxcarts with placards.
I moved through an embrasure cut in thick
adobe to the street and my parked car.

Time on Main

The Masonic Temple—white clapboard,
columns straight from some Egyptian opera set—
        began in resolution, but settled
to something jaunty, accomodating time.
        The stacked, half-cocked steeple's clock
permanently stopped at quarter past twelve.
        Noon? Midnight? Whatever;
it has two accurate moments,
        a kind of achievement,
after all these years. The living Masons
        must be few, and wise,
here in the plain north, to keep
        a staunch white meeting house
to disguise their treasury
        of costume: luscious get-ups,
staffs and turbans and robes,
        the ritual fabrics of dream.
Three steeples rise from Main Street's sleep
        cloudward (each of them pointless):
the Mason's frame homage to Luxor,
        the Congregationalist's dour stack,
and this: above arched windows
        inscribed, in marbled glass,
LOOK UP, a little Delphi's hung
        against the sky, twelve columns
squared around an open shaft
        of pure New England air.

Then a spate of retail, equally dreamy:
        a new trinket shoppe,
Gifts for the Soul. Black block letters
        —BRAD'S HOUSE OF TIME—
ring a neon clock. In the cemetery,

a hillock where two routes
converge, flat slate markers lean
          in rows, delicately inscribed:
urns and winged skulls, willows
          bent in perennial grief.
Answered, somehow, by one man's
          stone engraved in cursive
with a motto and farewell:
          It's all right. Time,
I'd like to think he meant,
          his hour, and ours, here in Egypt,
Vermont, Greece. Imagine
          thinking the passage of time
all right! A proposition this town
          considers still, all night long,
the moon a delicious frazzle
          in the rapids by the shut-down
mill, caught like Main
          in one continuous dream,
riddled with history, and outside it,
          sending these spires up
into October, year after year,
          at quarter past the hour.

The Lover's Face in Santa Cruz

Strange how the mind is. There is rain in the middle of the day
with light behind the drops on the windows. All afternoon
a different look on my face. Then Potenza, that strange
child, sees me in the bathroom mirror,
starts raving about the look on my face. In the Albion Store
her mom's boyfriend spoke of mirrors leaking. Leaking
dreams. The other side of this world is always leaking
into this one and we are always leaking into it. Embarrassed
I had to lie down. But now the quiet, the dark, all the room
going on without me. Suddenly I'm on a sunsplashed city street
in Santa Cruz riding in a car with you, seeing you crystal clear, framed
in the driver's window, seeing another
miraculous thing about you. You're the same
with all people, you don't leak. You carry your quiet,
sensitive self to everyone, to all situations equally.
I'm so impressed I understand what you were saying at Sanctuary
Station, how I change faces, personalities, energy
with whomever I'm with. I always thought this
was holy alchemy, how can one not be altered by the Other?
This morning talking with Loretta in Los Angeles with her dying mother
I was clownish, witty, cracking jokes. Few people
know this person. I who know no jokes. She always
elicits this from me, even with her mother so sick. I've always
called this love. Different people plug me into different currents,
for instance you. But now seeing your face in Santa Cruz
I hear those ugly expressions. Two-faced. Changing face. About-face.
Rising up that first hill from the store with the girls and groceries,
the money finally coming, the whole world is gorgeous, the wind
blowing great sunlight over the backs of the sheep, over everything
and I'm remembering how tender some of our moments have been
and I'm in bed with you under the window after a day of separation
in body and soul and heart and mind and the next thing I know
you are crying and then I'm holding our baby and you are talking

to me. Your steady tenderness is a miracle in my life. I see
you really would be my husband for life. What I've always wanted,
what I gave up in order to keep loving men. I have entered
the scene with our baby so totally it is with a start
I come out of it as we pass the barns. Then amazed at what I just did.
Is this the way some always are in their minds? When my husband
obsessed on sexual fantasies? When he was totally taken, totally
gone to another place, to other women? Some would say they've left
this body and really were with you on some Santa Cruz street.
That there really is a baby. Is this not love? I can't figure
out my face tonight, the Moon and Sun conjunct
in it. In this moment. In this room. Love, I am searching
for the way to tell you to leave me. Pray
I will always leak.

Ninety-Nine

The ninety-nine-year-old man
wants his son to collect popsicle sticks
and glue very fine sandpaper to them
in his spare time. The ninety-nine-year-old man
doesn't like the emery boards
at the nursing home. The son explains
he has no spare time
but what he means is that he has no inclination
to go to a hardware store
and risk having the cashier ask,
"Do you mean fine as in 'expensive'
or fine as in 'not coarse'?"
He has no inclination to discuss
such a time-consuming project with a store owner
who's used to men who build decks or shelves or counters.
He has no inclination to feel
the guilt of wishing his father would stop
busying him with these details, would stop
living all together so that he would stop
entering Ed McMahon sweepstakes.

Last year, the ninety-nine-year-old man
ordered a five year subscription
to *Runner's World Magazine* which will carry him
into the next century. He's hoping
that buying magazines will increase his chances
for winning big and getting out
of the nursing home once and for all.
This time he's ordered *Playboy*, not knowing
what it is until it arrives with his other mail.
He tells a nurse, "I'm not paying for this smut!
I'm ninety-nine, for Christ's sake,
what do I need this for?" He doesn't remember

checking just any old box just to enter the sweepstakes.
He doesn't remember where he's put his glasses.
He doesn't remember the M&M's his wife used to hide
in her lipstick, one on top of the other like beads.
He doesn't remember her rings which she lined up
in toaster slots so he couldn't toast his frozen waffles anymore.
He barely remembers the way she used to stare
into the fire on the stove, sticking her hand toward it
as though she'd forgotten all those meals she'd cooked,
as though she'd forgotten what fire actually was.

The ninety-nine-year-old man
looks at the centerfold trying to remember
the soft particulars of his wife's body,
but feels nothing in his loins like he used to.
He tries to remember what's next—
supper or lunch, pudding or Jello,
chipped beef or pot pie. Something like a cloud
of indigestion swirls around his heart.
But worst of all, his nails keep snagging his blanket.

Listening for Hooves, Catching Glimpses of the Red Hat That Was Never There

Maybe it's the listening that matters, standing on the linoleum of my kitchen, sponging hot chocolate rings off the table and pausing, leaning a little into the silence to catch them—hooves I am listening for. Listening for hooves that aren't there. Listening for them. Horse-galloping time, the tick tick of this listening in silence and leaning into what might be coming. Something is coming. Something always is, coming toward me out of the white haze of next, the distant next coming toward me on a great white that isn't there, traveling the trajectory of time from the sky it vanishes into, traveling back to me waiting, leaning, stopped in the act of cleaning what remains of the morning. Something is surely coming on hooves, on the sound of hooves, the pounding and drumming of hooves I stand still listening for, coming now out of the white that I am. Listening. And filled with the enormity of what is about to arrive, about to burst out of the foreseeable into now. Then my eyes see the blue sponge, the chocolate ring I intended to wipe, the marks on the linoleum and the uneven autumn light through the window. Maybe it came and went. Maybe it came and I missed it, and that explains my standing here bumping about in the flutter of things to do, things my hands and feet are doing. Maybe it's out there still, approaching, always and never arriving, and I just stopped listening, and it's gone. And that's why everything in the room, everything here in the world is a dull blow of disappointment, a little dull blow of something like despair. And this is what comes of listening that hard. This is what comes, of course, of listening for hooves, catching glimpses of what was never there.

Meeting Adjourned

The chairman raps his mahogany gavel.
The committee rises with a decorous scraping of chairs
and files out murmuring. It has been agreed:
there is so little time and so much to be done.

There will arise the inevitable protests,
the usual cranks to be courted or threatened by turns.
But it has been agreed:
whatever must be done will be done.

They descend the marble staircase in a body
and saunter into the street.
A volley of lead-grey doves
bursts from the portico like a spatter of shrapnel.

With one accord, the committee inspects their sky,
a faded denim patch on emptiness,
then nod to one another in common consent,
solemn, consequential, confident,

smug as a fistful of change in a shopkeeper's pocket.

Loosestrife Watch

The Natural History Section is calling a Purple Loosestrife Watch.
                                        Missouri Conservationist

On wind, on water, on the supple webs
of teal and mallard, they're moving in,
purpling the wetlands. No bird, nor porcupine,
nor woodchuck munches their tapering leaves.
Though possum, waddling the roadside ditch,
does nibble their softly spiring clusters,
then absent-mindedly carries their dust
away on his whiskers to greener pastures.

If you see some, please let us know.

Their imperturbable magenta
lulls the flood plain. They may be meek,
they may be comely, but they're moving in.
One more possum-load of pollen,
and there goes the neighborhood.

Father's Day

In the white-hot weather
In this welter of August

My father sheds his shell,
Steps out of his tabernacle

Of skin and into the gravest
Of summer afternoons, now,

Seen strolling over the varied
Crimsons of a limitless rainbow

Road, like the kind he would have
Admired on the Route 66 horizon

Covers of *Arizona Highways* that,
Still, show shadows of my father's

Generation asleep in these loud
Silences of a lost mirage; tourist

Donkey rides to the floor of the
Grand Canyon, with winking cameras

And here's a pretty picture: back
Where my father was born, there's

A funeral of cement—lilacs
Border the walks in Winnetka

A Grandmother Drops Distantly from on High

It is too far to the side of
Night; how she dreams, now, in her
Highest hours, how pitiful in her
Final sleep

It's as if an entire family's funeral
Watch weeps, in order to give more time
To her thirsty heart

Everything that keeps us safe, in the
Sight of what we call nature,
Falls
With the force of a snowstorm

But, there is no snow, no bright, no
Delicate, no melting thing anywhere,
That, eventually, disappears,
As precious as she has been

And you really never knew, before this,
That there was anywhere she could go
Without taking you along

Inside, where a fireplace rages, a
Winter's cache of relatives
Gives up her warm ghost

Outside, there's only that cold cry of the rain

PATRICIA GOEDICKE

Third Rail
(Autobiography of Lastness)

Because they are two old birds—
telling each other they are one.

Because they are not,
because they are more than one, and disintegrating

like a swarm of insects, brown midges over water
fizzing into the sun and then out, in the blink of an eye

all brightness gone and nobody left but *us chickens*:

plucked, exhausted.
Left on the counter too long.

Because we had to rest
sometime, because—

(nothing.)

Scooped from each other's skin like cold potatoes

that got lost, that couldn't find their way home.

See, there is this third rail running underneath us.
That won't go away, that wants to slice us into pieces.

In the middle of the most innocuous remark it leaps out at her—
No, it leaps out at him. Like a dog on a leash, snarling.

Down girl, down.

Sharks on the prowl veer
toward her feet, electricity swooshes through the dark.

"No, dear, the car keys aren't in the sugar bowl!"
she snaps: but couldn't this be funny?

Sarcasm, get out of my mouth.

Because she thought she could carry both of them
all the way into the kitchen.

> Because she couldn't, because the high C of self-
> hatred spiders over cracked windshields—

And still she cracks it, the hissing whip of her guilt
all around him, *crack, crack*—

> Oh, she is shameless. Smart as a shoe with a pebble in it;
> here's gravel in her eye.

Every remark has its edge:

> Scratch others scratch yourself
> she knows.

She wants to forgive herself, can't:

> *O poisonous bee, tail that turns on itself*
> (in the blaming that is marriage).

As the rail slices by beneath them, the San Andreas Fault secretly
stirs in everyone's midriff

> *but mine especially,* she insists (all of us
> clutch at ourselves and insist)—

Because she only wanted to be one with him
forever. (See, it was never her fault).

> Because there are two of them,
> after all. And no one's to blame, *no one*

> that finally everyone forgets,

> that fire ants sizzle in our heads,
> that synapses break down and ooze

acid none of us can stomach:
tangles nests of neurons, black

sparks spitting at each other along the crack

that was there from the beginning,

in the cell as soon as it was born
forever fractured, even along the dividing

invisible line between the two halves
of the doubled cerebellum......

Because it's all in their heads?

And then he erupts at her,
who else?

Shouts, hot lava boils over the stove

and out the front door: "I won't be back
you'll see me when you see me"—

But inside her forever.

Yet she can barely hear him
over the burglar-alarm shrieking

that won't stop, that drills through the entire neighborhood
like a needle but what's missing?

Nothing's stolen that belonged
to either one of them.

Oh, maybe a few brain cells, a couple of old tapes
trashed. Scrambled. Discarded on the back seat.

But not by her, never! She swears at herself, Radio Signal:

Emergency. Program Over.

What we gave up for each other, they think,

our own shores invaded until we are one
country with no borders, Help.

       Because they are falling apart
       together, falling apart

they keep picking at each other; stop, go,

             as she makes lists for him, draws maps
             which he objects to, or she does—

Anxiety churns the waters: red bacteria chewing
all up and down the eastern seaboard.

       So they retreat, almost back to the beginning

they curl in their bed in the dark, grown couple murmuring
nonsense at each other, the sheer babble

       and comfort of mindlessness together—

But sometimes the rail loops upwards, climbing a hill.

       Vein of viciousness, grim zipper whipping by—
       which never moves, watch out!

       Because we are one body.
Birthing itself. Into pieces.

       The secret conductor of shock slithers through the water,

       the jagged current slashes
       between us but we are manacled together,

welded, then broken. Fused, but only until the final
infinite division:

       the diaspora of stars

---

those cut-outs of darkness, shattered pieces of light

reflections only: in scraps of paper, in snapshots
in the brief minds of friends

   arguing together, like streams in their beds muttering, in the low
   backtalk of lives going by—

Because we are more than one, and disintegrating:

   birthing ourselves into pieces.

Rage, rage, go away.
All the bright oranges are bleeding.

   O but the one face

out of all others, the rolling voice like a bell buoy
still tugs at her guts, harbor she can't get out of

   and doesn't want to:

because the body lives
by definition only:
   inside its own borders and banging at them.

Outside there's nothing, *no thing*
but air the prickling skin shivers against

   to protect what's underneath it:

the dim, private rasp
and gurgle of blood, the seven stopped orifices

   choked, cliffed,
   like the sea beating against dry land

   even as they crumble together, *Hold my hand*

   ―――――――――

she whispers, in the cry of seagull and rooster,
in the loud spittle of foam,

—*"nor eye has seen, nor ear heard"*—

in the roar of the shadowy spirit breaking up

> that won't go away without fighting,
> *on the edge*

> of evil that was always there, the cell dividing
> and splitting away from itself, into infinity multiplying

as we who were one body

> > *from the beginning* seem to seperate
> > into farther and farther waters,

> > as earth breaks itself up

into sorrow on all sides, into pain,
into meaner and meaner fractions,

> cavities our sniping tongues
> keep *picking* at

as if anyone could stop it, the cruel snake
and piecemeal of stars chipping themselves away

> high above us, in the light
> that is all around us, under the crack in the door

at the bottom of the sea, in the fierce, unknowable
heave of wave and quantum

> pulsing heavily upwards, *Where are you*

> she cries out and keeps on crying

as all that is inside *is dispersed*, shimmering
in the spume of a thousand eyes,

> interminably flowing, in veiled phosphorescencies turning

> and turning on themselves, wave on wave........

The Weather Channel

Hast thou, spirit, perform'd to point
the tempest I bade thee?
—Prospero

John announces he wishes
he'd invented The Weather Channel,
the highest ratings during a disaster.
He relaxes after work,
a job with no glamour.
Now Blanco, Henly, Dripping Springs
are under the radar's
deep sweeping green
spotted orange and yellow,
the advisory in bleeps and stars
telling us to avoid windows
since this system
already has a history
of damage. Frannie is buried
in terriers on the couch
while counseling Mary
on winter pruning.
Erin is speaking to the heavens
on her new pink phone,
and her brother Jason is gone
in a thick mystery,
a dead woman
all but naked on its cover.
The system is now
just west of Austin,
and as if to dare it
John bets it won't come here.
The wind stirs
the darkening branch
over the house he built

with his own hands,
while Ariel, Erin's little gray tiger,
is poised to attack
the draft in the tall
white curtain.

High Pressure

It's 11:30 p.m., and the temp
Is holding at 91 degrees.
For hours, a hound has been howling
Like he wants to swallow
The full moon;
The crickets' chirr is an axe
To split the night in two.
My coastal friends—
The cool bastards—
Do not understand that we,
Here in the lowlands,
Are called to a higher duty,
To nights of wet pillows
And days of glare and no glory
But the getting through.
When it's 106, we mow our lawns:
We believe in practicing for hell.
But it's not the hound and the crickets
That have me riled and sleepless,
And it's not the solitude
I've carried through the years
Like it was my *curriculum vitae.*
Conrad said, "...solitude loses its terrors
Once one fully knows it."
No, it's the photo I saw this morning,
Taken in Sudan.
A man has stolen a bag of food
From a starving child.
The boy, though long limbed,
Can't weigh more that 30 pounds.
He is on all fours,
Likely too weak to stand,
And he stares not at the man

In the white robe,
But at the hand that has just seized
The white plastic bag of food.
I say these two things are white
As though that detail means something,
But what would it matter
If the robe were cerise or fuschia or puce?
This happens in a place
That makes symbolism seem
Like a mockery of human suffering,
A place of equatorial heat;
The boy's knees and palms must be on fire.
What is important about the robe
Is that it is spotless and soft looking
And unwrinkled, as if the man
Has a fresh robe for each day of the week.
You will believe me when I say
That nothing has prepared me for this hell.
I can't get past the picture;
I can't go around it or through it.
It belongs to me now,
Another item in my c.v.,
Something to carry not conquer,
And it changes the way I look at the other hell.
If when I get there I will meet
This white-robed man with a conscience
So ingrown that it imploded,
And if I will be allowed to watch
As the hounds of hell
Spend eternity tearing him to shreds,
Flinging out gobbets of flesh
To the cackling jackals and vultures,
Then I will go there almost with eagerness,
And I will bear its heat,
And it will be for me a place of glory.

On Turning 55

This year, mysteriously,
Has been the year of the toad.
On any night, all summer,
I could sweep the yard
With the flashlight
And find half a dozen young ones
Bumbling over the grass.
It's almost the end of my birth day,
And it's cool for an August night
In this boiler of a valley.
Only a solitary cricket
Arias below the window.
Do toads eat crickets?
The question requires that extra
Splash of whiskey
My mind tells me
I should not allow myself.
My mind, my mind.
Mostly we've made our peace,
But it still troubles me
With advice I can't take.
It used to be sharp,
It used to remember everything,
Even the names of people,
But now it's turning into something
Suspiciously like a conscience,
A word too many of my students
Want to spell as conscious.
Very well, my conscious bothers me,
But my unconscience has been subdued.
Once, turning the compost pile,
I stabbed a buried toad
Through its very center with the pitchfork.
It twitched on the tine,
And fluid ran out of its abdomen.
I closed my eyes

And shook it off into the trash can
And wished there was a way
To keep things out of the memory,
Which is sometimes not a bank
Where the teller passes out delights
When your turn comes at last
But a vault of horrors,
And this is where the fear lies:
What if good memories fade first,
Dropping away like names,
And one is left with pitchforks,
Toads, solitary singers,
A mind held captive
By its guilts,
Grimacing with closed eyes?

February Snow and Star Songs

In curled snow
allegrettos, Belgian lace.
Trees grow birds.
Black roses, grackles drop
rough notes against pure blue—
Immaculata Conceptio,
Mary not contrary,
a notion of heaven.

The choppy syntax
of the windswept river,
glottal stopped on mud,
gathers over pocked snow
in the church yard
of Santa Maria Josepha,
Daughter of Mercy,
exemplar of patience.

My Sister's veiny face, a rose.
When snow turned to pools,
children sang: "There was a ship
that sailed and sailed . . ."
Juice she tipped to my mouth
to cool a fevered throat,
sloshed and gurgled,
an orange sea in my hidden coves,

and my spirit was a ship
pulled by the tide of bells
from the tower.
Allegro. Allegro.
Mary Mother, at that hour
prayed for us under a sky

that would crisscross
with white stars, conjugating

who we were, now are, they are, we are
nothing without them,
and my fever sailed away.

Busboy Kills Goliath

The stunning busboy in the ptomaine
trattoria on 19th street
pours olive oil into a dish near
our bread, frozen in the pose
of Caravaggio's "David with
the Head of Goliath," his long-lashed
eyes lowered modestly
at the havoc he has wreaked
on the beheaded thyroid freak
who dared admire the lips
of the angry youthful beauty
already worried about his tip.

Elevator at the Modern Art Museum

Imprisoned cricket,
the elevator shrieking at each floor
bears an oblong attendant
squatting on a stool,
her Danielle Steel clutched
to heavy thigh, going
up and down at the
Soho retrospective of an artist
who denied he was gay
and spent good money to
reconstruct his nose,
after cocaine did what
posterity someday may.

Massage Parlor Days

She was standing across the desk
        from her ex-con manager
who just accused her of stealing
        a vibrator. This is crazy,

she thought, although it was not,
        it made a crude sense.
Old Town townhouse, three stories
        and a half-basement,

every room—ceilings, walls, floors,
        the glass and frames of windows—
painted black, psychedelic posters
        glowing in blacklight

and patchouli and sandalwood,
        smells that seemed antique
and unending, a touch that linked them
        to their kind worldwide,

the seamy side no matter the century,
        the wild glide, hand job,
blow job, anything-you-can-name,
        the kinky included,

bizarre or pathetic, dangerous
        or tender, repressed appetites
unleashed, or whipped into existence.
        She worked the dayshift,

mostly businessmen between flights.
        They'd taxi over then taxi back.
Safe, stodgy-faced men who wanted
        to prove they could step out

of line on occasion; the meek,
        drunken and brazen, all charged
for Feather, or Swedish, or Hot Oil,
        or Oriental, the hand roll,

roll-the-dice, slow show,
        double whammy, name-the-act
mystery prize. Runaways or deserted
        mothers, trailer park girls

or downtown tenement, parent-
        or uncle- or neighbor-abused,
the emergency room their only
        physician, not one

with straightened teeth—Delilah,
        Delphine, Davana, Jasmine—
sugar for sugar daddies,
        suckers for drug addicts.

They worked at sex standing up
        as if it held them fixed.
Business slow they'd gossip and tell
        their kicked-out, slapped-around

stories, girls with flash without a speck
        of self-respect, the wrist-slashed,
overdosed but didn't-die discards
        using their mouths and hands,

breasts and cunts because that was
        what they had. *Why would
I steal your fucking vibrator?* she
        screamed. But it was whiny

bitching crap to him so with the back
        of his hand he smacked her off.
I'm taking my cut and your cut,
        he said, and that was that.

Unholy Sonnet

History happening and people living
While you are not. And as for your non-presence,
Nobody knows of it or needs you yet.
People alive in life and history happening.
And where you will be one day: plenty of space
And time, like fractions deep inside of pi,
The genes of its irrationality,
Just waiting for division to locate them.
Wherever you fit, elbowing your survival
Into its niche of habit and surprise,
A handful of machines that share your codes,
And would spill blood to save them, will surround you.
Meanwhile, between the egg and sperm—oblivion,
Gossip of sweet delight and endless night.

Epilogue

Today is fresh, and yesterday is stale.
Today is fast, and yesterday is slow.
Today is yes, and yesterday is no.
Today is news, and yesterday's a tale.
The grave is empty. Last night it was full.
The glorious means of death was once a shame.
Someone is God who had a common name
That you might give a child or animal.
It happens overnight. The world is changed.
The bottles in the cellar all decant.
The stars sign the new cosmos at a slant.
And everybody's plans are rearranged.
Today we meet our maker, in a flash
That turns the ash of yesterday to flesh.

Variations

I

Sonya sits at the piano, practicing.
She yearns for what does not exist, it seems,
Something beyond all music; and to her
The whole pathos of chromaticism seems
      A purely mechanical exercise.
      And yet she sighs and does not know why she sighs.

II

So at reunions, recognizing the songs,
We feel at one with the sadness of our class.
The singing spreads, spreads and becomes general—
O ineluctable blues of the middle class!
      Softly we sing, and the more forgetful hum.
      Time the River, Time the Destroyer! Yes, ho hum.

III

Glorious to be away from the mill at last!
On such a day the sky looks strangely poetic
With all the sad poetry of chimney and of gable.
To the young poet, of course, everything looks poetic—
      The clouds, the vast white Saturday afternoon,
      Yes, even the grimy mill-men tavern-bound at noon.

His Last Unpublished Poem

Contributor's Note

His date of birth,
His occupations,
His residence,
His publications—

The latest news
Of him is ripe
To be perused
In six-point type.

No mention of
Those he betrayed
The lack of love,
The thoughts that fade.

Unmentioned are
His eyes, his breath,
His hidden scar,
And wish for death.

Note: The above poem survived only by accident in a college report written in August,1940 by Charles M. Lightfoot, a student at Northwestern University. Lightfoot had met Kees two years earlier in the Denver Public Library. In 1940 Lightfoot decided to do his class project in a course entitled "The Interpretation of Contemporary American Poetry", on Kees, whose first book, *The Last Man* (1943) had not yet appeared. Lightfoot wrote the poet for information and included a list of questions mandated by the instructor. Kees responded by answering the questions and enclosing a bibliography as well as several unpublished poems. All of the poems were eventually published except for "Contributor's Note," which seems to have been written as a sardonic comment on the student's long list of questions about the poet's life and opinions. Kees claimed that he destroyed about half of the poems he wrote in the years between 1937 and 1940 (when he shifted his interests from fiction to verse). "Contributor's Note" seems inadvertently to have survived destruction. Kees destroyed his copy of the poem but kept a carbon of Lightfoot's report, which he had requested as the price of his participation.

—*Dana Gioia*

In the Night

There are spirit presences
Around my bed
Waiting for me to die.
They are in no great hurry
Nor am I.

Do not fear death
I whisper to my keepers.
Fear life if it goes on too long.
For the lost losers
Make winners weepers.

It's so quiet tonight
I can hear the angels breathing.
Our hands are transparent,
As veined as autumn leaves.
I rest in their arms
And sense the mist rising.

Trio

Some say sorrow fades.
I shall carry my sorrow forever
Long after I smile farewell
To those who leave me here.
Always tears because
Only joy endures.
Joy remains in the mind
As do those who made us glad
In a moment of light forever.

My mother, my first two lovers,
One tall and fair—a friend;
One fearful, swart and tired,
Antagonist to the end.
My mother, tall and fair,
Afraid of death and weather,
Fearful and glad together!
What silence shakes the mind
Now it has lost your way,
Your full, consoling laughter!

Now that your light has gone out,
A long long light remains.
I weather into age
Mourning the brave and kind.
I pace the days along,
Three shadows follow after:
Two who were tall and fair
Are carolling behind,
And a third, who had no song.

A Day in the Life

Dr. X (not his real name) and I (not my real name) got together,
        so to speak, when I was in Tucson on sabbatical
and my back stiffened up. So I looked for a chiropractor in the phone
        book and found one nearby. I've seen my share over
the years, and his approach was a little tender, but something
        popped and I was about to pay him when he threw
in a free massage. It was hot in Tucson. I had on shorts and a T-
        shirt and soon I added an erection to that ensemble
as he massaged both faster and yet more tenderly until he asked
        politely if he could relieve the new stiffness and I said,
"Better hurry."

        I walked home and told my wife, not like tattling
or confessing even but just recounting an interesting afternoon
        in what was a fine but also uneventful sabbatical.
"Did you like it enough for me to worry?" she asked? And I
        said, "No, I don't think so." Because I liked it well
enough, but not his aftershave or what used to be called a
        five o'clock shadow. I did like feeling seduced, though:
the caresses, the woozy feeling, the denial that anything, really,
        was happening. And though I was never a cad or what
my wife called a big creep-a-roni, I'd done my share of aggressive
        caressing and general mesmerizing in order to get
where I thought I wanted to be. So I felt a sudden kinship with
        all those girls in cars and graduate housing and on
blankets and balconies and once standing up in the bathroom of
        an ARCO station. In fact, I felt more than a kinship.
I felt like a woman.

        That night in bed, my wife was sweeter than usual and
even what you might call competitive, but since I felt like a woman
        I wondered if that meant she was having a homosexual
experience, too. A lot of people were. Lesbians poured into town

from Colorado, opened a food co-op and flirted with
the shoppers who were so flattered they took the kids and moved
        out to a sprawling commune near Tanque Verde.
We were one of a very few couples who went to a party together
        and left together instead of with another man
or woman (or both) and a book with the word *Joy* in the title.

About midnight, not even bothering to get dressed,
we got some beers and went out on the patio to try and cool off.
        "Are we okay?" I asked. And she replied, "Sure. What else did
you do today?" So I told her about washing the car and she
        told me about her job at a health food store where
people came in every day looking for happiness, probably, and settled
        for calcium or a B-complex. In a few years we'd fall,
as they say, out of love and be mean to one another but that night we
        were interested in our lives again. I could see the need
for novelty and even the attraction of mutiny, but I didn't want to
        think about it. I wanted to watch the way the wind
dried her hair and be happier than ever knowing not only that it could
        end, but probably would.

Old & Neglected

Of course nobody ever calls them
that because they were willing
extras in the movie, sidekicks
for the handsome and charismatic,
donkey, ox, and dromedary
in the crèche of poetry.

Willing to the end, they stand
on the platform waving good-bye
to the new & selected, passing
lunches through the window,
even playing in the band, sweating
in the scratchy uniforms.

And when that streamliner
has pulled away, their train chugs
up. Next stop Obscurity, where
it's always June, couples must walk
hand in hand toward a twenty-four
hour sunset, and everyone lives
beside a warm, slow-moving river
that nevertheless overflows
its banks every Mother's Day.

Oil Lamp

Its chimney is the silence surrounding
a little pipe organ that shimmers on top of the wick
with no one to play it, or can that be a choir
in golden robes, waiting to sing? Whatever it is
it glows with silence and patience. A person
could sit here for hours, entranced and deceived,
believing that love, with a murmur of wings,
will eventually come to the window.

Dishwater

Slap of the screen door, flat knock
of my grandmother's boxy black shoes
on the wooden stoop, the hush and sweep
of her knob-kneed, cotton-aproned stride
out to the edge and then, toed in
with a furious twist and heave,
a bridge that leaps from her hot red hands
and hangs there shining for fifty years
over the mystified chickens,
over the swaying nettles, the ragweed,
the clay slope down to the creek,
over the redwing blackbirds in the tops
of the willows, a glorious rainbow
with an empty dishpan swinging at one end.

The China Painters

They have set aside their black tin boxes,
scratched and dented,
spattered with drops of pink and blue;
and their dried up, rolled up tubes
of alizarine crimson, chrome green,
zinc white and ultramarine;
their vials half full of gold powder;
stubs of wax pencils;
frayed brushes with tooth bitten shafts;
and have gone in fashion and with grace
into the clouds of loose, lush roses,
narcissus, pansies, columbine
on teapots, chocolate pots,
saucers and cups, the good Haviland dishes
spread like a garden
on the white lace Sunday cloth,
as if their souls were bees
and the world had been nothing but flowers.

Coal Stoker

That was my father's job, feeding the black tin bin
with scoops of coal when the auger had pushed the last load
into the flames. Then he'd lean on his shovel
and watch the glow through the flickering isinglass pane.
The furnace seemed huge, like my father's mother,
obese and complaining, upstairs in my sister's bed
where she'd come to mend her broken shoulder
but where she would die of a blood clot that formed
under a too-tight bandage. Mother fed her with soups
and diced up meat, creamed vegetables and pie
while the old woman burned with silent resentment
toward Mother for taking her son. I remember
that furnace's pipes, big sagging arms like Grandmother's.
They seemed to be holding up our crowded house,
but maybe they reached right through that creaking floor,
up through the roof and into the cold and waiting stars,
each pipe so tightly wrapped in white asbestos cloth.

A Distant Storm

When I die,
I wish that there might be
a flash
like that of lightning
as the past illuminates the room,
and then a pause,
and a darkening,
before the present thunders in.

Flashback

For Edward Field, Navigator

Our twenty-
seventh
bombing run,

flak
bursting
all around,

we're caught
in some gun's
eager sights.

Our own
gunner
is raving—

best pretend
not
to notice.

There goes
Chuck's plane
down—

please live,
Chuck, we shout
to the canopy.

As a child,
I knew
I'd never die.

Here though
is the
world our

beautiful
bodies
climbed up

to drop down
through
together,

not the
together
we wanted.

There,
another plane
falling.

Nothing
we
can
do.

Remembering James Merrill

What has happened keeps happening.
Take: a spring day nineteen seventy-nine.
JM has worked on the atom all morning
and is preparing lunch for the pilgrim
coming up Water Street with an offering
of wine the store man promised was okay.
The visitor wonders how he can say all
he needs to say and be ready to leave
by two o'clock, naptime in Stonington,
as everybody knows. Careful now, Jimmy,
slice the cucumber, not your finger:
Tonight you're to work on the little piece
by Satie. Doorbell! Pity the breathless
votary standing there. The door opens. . .

One Morning We Found

One morning we found the near
corner of the Long Meadow mowed
into six diamonds in the rough.
Cleated anticipation made a parade

of our walk over the grass arcs,
rippling out from the sandy base
lines. We could smell neat's-foot
oil and moments when we could live

in that pounded pocket of time
where all that matters seems so
clear, everyone watching breathes
together, as if life were caught

in that two out, full count torque,
converging on us, fast and true.

A Valediction Forbidding Mourning
for Larry Levis

I'm listening from my porch for the music
of eloquent Spanish insults
from your father's grape gleaners, Johnny and Angel.
I'm listening for the dust to crackle
over Vivaldi on vinyl in your father's dark room.
I'm listening to the chants of girls skipping rope because
I can't help it. It's the irony I like.
"We all fall down," sings to me right now
as sweetly as Monk's pinky finger
doing whatever he God damn wanted it to do,
1949, '59, '69, whatever.
"God damn it all," is what my father would bellow
when I'd come home at four in the morning.
After that, doors slammed shut and birds started singing.
He couldn't help it because he was listening for me.
I don't think he wanted to, but that was our ineffable pact,
congealing the blood,
which is all I'd say there is to sleep on.
So I'm going to go out to the corner with the girls
and I'm going to start talking to whoever will listen.
I'm going to tell them your stories and how they
show me how to pity myself, then to forget it.
I'm going to put my arm around the first guy who comes up to me
with a Louisville Slugger dangling from his left hand
and whisper in his ear that it is not only possible, but necessary
to make the grain in a desk or a bat confess
all the sorry incongruities of the gnostics
if you're ever really going to have a good time or find your way home.
Whoever's still around after that can come with me to McGlinchy's, 15th & Spruce,
even the rookie cop, and we'll do shots of ouzo or Cuervo,
and we'll toast your one wren that flew backwards
into eternity as a poem, and made it.

We'll break and sink nine-ball over and over.
Those who smoke can.
Those who need to call home should.
We'll call out from work if we have to,
we'll call out over the orchards of Parlier and all their white flags,
as if there were something to surrender to.
I'll get all the change we need for the juke box
and we'll sing, God damn it all, we're staying
and we're singing as long as we can stand it,
as long as our cracked and cracking voices,
like rotting angels, will let us.

Indian Summer Gives Way to the Land of the Rising Sun

Memory is malleable.
Memory is a scar.
Because all things return
to their source,
grace is possible.

***

Pine Ridge at dusk,
from a balcony of the IHS hospital,
clouds smoke above the dry earth.
They look real, like clouds in those
paintings, those oil landscapes by
that artist on PBS—that white guy
with an afro, the one who spoke
with a hillbilly drawl and used
two-inch house brushes to
daub his little masterpieces.
He died from cancer a while back,
but has been reborn in re-runs.

***

Darkness, sneaking Marlboros
on the balcony, bugs crawling
down the back of my hospital gown.
Under the parking lot light poles,
flying insects swarm, some able
to retain luminosity and fly
far away with it.
Fireflies? I don't know . . .
A young nurse from Ft. Berthold
says there are fireflies at her home,
but none down here in the wilds
of godless South Dakota.
She puts her hand to my cheek

to check on my fever and
I shudder with loneliness.
I wish I could take her hand
and pull her silently into
the motorized bed with me.
We could share the same cigarette.
The way I feel, it might be my last.

***

Indian macho:
If you're going to get shot,
you might as well have a Marlboro
dangling from your lips . . . ennit?
On the road below the hospital,
a young woman is running from
her drunk boyfriend. He pants,
swears and sweats up the hill
after her, but she is too fast,
too sober.

***

Days drag through the unseasonable
warmth of late fall that white
people call *Indian summer.*
It's Indian summer
all year long around here
and through my medicinal haze
I think I hear the nurse say she'll
cook me a steak when I heal.

Memory is malleable.
Memory is a scar.
Because all things return
to their source,
grace is possible.
The simple vision of a brown
woman cooking over a stove is
a good reason to live.
But I get no steak. Instead, she

thrusts a tube up my nose and
then down into my stomach.
Ghastly brown liquid bubbles
into a glass cauldron.
I thrash and moan and wonder
who those green men are who
sit at the foot of my bed.

***

I am entering a faraway land.
The Indian Health Service ambulance
bumps along the dirt road, exhaust
fumes filling this tin can where I lie
like a fat sardine upon the bed, stench
from the exhaust choking, my stomach
in flames, I'm feverish, the smoking
ambulance rips down the road and up
towards Rapid City like something out
of a Road Runner cartoon.
Then, I'm in Regional Hospital.
The surgeon says the x-rays look
like colon cancer. She smiles.
I smile back and wink and
resign myself to my clichéd fate.
I am entering a faraway land.
For all I know, it could be Japan.

***

There are weeks that I know nothing
about when my kidneys shut down,
when my lungs shut down, when
I nearly pass on to the spirit world.
There's no bright light, I do not float
above my bed, but Colleen, you keep
coming back to me, your sweet softness,
the innocent mist you're in now,
this reservation where I found you,
where I look for you, where I cannot

find you, the past, the present all mixed,
mixed in this faraway land, and you're
so soft, wearing a long blue skirt, so soft
and so lost and your family is taking
care of you since I cannot now . . .
but as usual, they're not doing
a good job and they lose you.

***

Somehow the idea comes to write
a book with paintings, watercolors
of Mexican peasant plates, each plate
will tell a story. It's bizarre, but I see
myself forward, out of the hospital
and healing. I'll set up an easel in my
backyard and paint the pictures.
Even in my sickness, I know it's a
crazy idea, but then for a month I waver
between madness and extreme madness.
I believe I have cancer though the doctors
tell me daily that I don't. The thing that
sustains me, keeps me going, is apple juice.
Apple juice grows in the basement of
the hospital where old Jewish women
squeeze the sweet wetness from gray mud.
They dribble it into vials—I drink it and
my life continues. And in this basement
people float like balloons near the ceiling
and one of these people is a little monkey
dressed in a black suit and top hat.
He wears a beard and glasses.
This monkey talks to me.
I don't know why, but I believe
it is a Japanese monkey.
He screams: PEARL HARBOR!
And my mad Mexican plates fly
around the room and smash
to smithereens.

***

Every imaginable type of ghost
is dancing in my room.
I'm sick and stoned beyond stone.
Toxic encephalopathy.
My brain, my entire body is poisoned.
I am a toxic half-breed!
A loony and languid viper
hissing on the doorsteps of hell.

Hank Williams is under my bed
singing "Rambling Man" and I've
got plastic tubes up my penis
and down my throat, in my wrist
and chest and somach. A huge
stitched trench runs from my
solar plexus to my belly button.
My American river of madness
pisses against all reason, flowing east
from Rapid City to St. Paul and then
into Cambridge, Mass. All three
cities merge into brick sameness.
There's a small tavern in the fog
named the *Ribeltad Vorden* or maybe
the *Plough and Stars* and it's filled
with derelicts, Indians, and artists.
I buy a pint of good Irish whiskey
and drop it in the pocket of my raincoat
where it clinks up against a chrome .45
and my brother-in-law Duane is there
in an ill-fitting, itchy tweed suit.
Duane's a tribal detective so I ask
if the Japanese doctors who implanted
the golden wire from the base of my brain
to my coccyx have cured the cancer
and he says yeah, hell yeah.
I give him the chrome automatic and tell
him I plan to give one to all his brothers.

And how is sweet-crazy Colleen I ask.
Waiting, he says. She's waiting for you.

                    ***

The flights to Japan were killers.
And the Japanese not only cured me,
but they harvested a kidney
without my permission.
Like it was me
who raised the flag
on Iwo Jima . . .

The jets were long and lean lungfish.
I was the only rider on most trips.
The aisles were windswept and cellophane
overhead ran the length of the plane.
A howling wind whooshed the plastic
making me cry each time we landed.
On one flight, an ancient lover, now gray
and beaten, sat behind me and drooled.
She said they stole her kidney too.
Said she was a bag lady now!
That it was all my fault.

                    ***

Strange, how it took me a month
to believe I didn't have cancer,
and had never been to Japan.
They did remove a huge chunk
of my colon and gave me a colostomy
bag that I'd have to wear for six smelly
months, but I never had cancer,
I never had the fucking Big C . . .

I didn't, did I?

                    ***

Somewhere in this airless
examining room I can almost

hear my young red-headed surgeon
and her young surgeon husband
doing the dirty deed atop
this Danish modern furniture.
It's now been one year since surgery.
My vibrant MD enters, all smiles, and
says, "You're lookin' good!" But, there
are many other things she tells me,
as she looks at my chart, things I do not
recall at all like how I stood atop my
bed and screamed I was a poet.
How I ripped loose my colostomy
bag and beaned a nurse with it.
How they tied me down for weeks,
stuck a tube down my soul,
and fed me life.

I'm embarrassed, but I am alive.
I thank the spirits for deleting
those memories. One of these
days I just might fly to Japan
and thank those doctors.
Domo arigato!
Sushi?
Banzai!
Remember Pearl Harbor?

Femme Fatale

It's a crime story she's in:
betrayal and larceny, few clues.
Someone stole what she lived for,
made off like a thief in the night
or high noon. What shall she do?
Put a heel on each foot and set out,
making a snapping sound as she steps.
The man she loves smiles
from the drugstore's rack
of magazines, just in.
Looks like he's wrapped his movie,
dropped his wife on a Frisian Island
and is flying his girlfriend to St. Tropez.
The men who love her finger coins
in the stale linings of their front
pockets and whimper *What's your name?*
The job she wanted went
to the man who tells the truth
from one side of his mouth, lies
from the other: a bilingual.
The job she got lets her
answer the questioning phone all day.
Her disappointment has appetite,
gravity. Fall in, you'll be crunched
and munched, stretched
thin as fettuccine. Watch out for her,
this woman, there is more than one.
That woman with you, for instance,
checking herself in the mirror
to see where she stands—
she's innocent so far, but someone
will disappoint her.
Even now you're beginning to.
Even now you're in danger.

Whore

It comes from *hore* in Old English.
Hora in Old Norwegian.
But the Latin references charity.
At the root it's *carus*—dear,
as in *Hello, whore. Hello, dear.*
As in loved one, sweetheart, precious,
as in rare—therefore expensive, dear,
cher, cheri, a luxury
when given freely
pitting charity against law.

Coyote Couple

Where once two shadows sharp
and dark as obsidian slashed
the moon-scoured desert floor
a single silhouette now ripples
across rock, ironwood and mesquite,
bits of bleached bone: He
in her shade? She in his? Who knows?

Or if apart, each alive
to the other's whiff, sigh, footfall,
ululation, as though these formed
the tensile threads of a common
language, tugging toward union, tugging
toward fusion: a new element
forged out of gold mine's slag.

The coupling of creatures blesses
the earth with new being: still self
and self yet an other, too, each
with one eye turned outward
to the world, the other in where
gaze meets gaze, somber, mute,
though remembering ever how
to cavort, how in the dark to sing.

DIONISIO D. MARTÍNEZ

The Prodigal Son Bribes the Fortune Teller

"Dust off the superlatives and the leather vest. Prepare for another onslaught of arcane proportions. Here, get a handle on the new filing system before assuming your assigned position. The news leaks so rarely, and the little that seeps out is strictly second-rate material; what you get is a mirroring of the news, moisture building on the outside of a milk bottle. A reading of barometric pressure is always open to interpretation, like playing the 'Gentlewoman attending on Lady Macbeth' or conducting the premiere of an unfinished quartet with a series of optional bassoon interludes. They know you by your accounts of cultural trends—hush money, a flurry of distress signals—but they only remember your role in the highly acclaimed scandal. Proving that not all matter has substance is simple if you know your way back to the vacuum. Take a dowsing rod or a wishbone. You hear the sound of one shoe creaking as you walk; you stop and the sound continues. A sense-deprivation retreat will do you good. It's late Monday morning—the slate wiped bare with snake oil—before you know what hit you."

The Prodigal Son in His Own Words:
Prayer Against *Ecclesiastes*

Budding leaves on a dying tree. *Alpha* like a grain on the tongue.
The first and only word. A sigh. Under this sun each thing is new
and incomplete. Water from melting snow doesn't flow out of sight
in shame. Another school of salmon answers the gravitational pull
of a heavy sky. Even our losses are fresh: in its finite wisdom each
thing—virginity, a good crop—leaves a taste of itself: the last and
only absence and *alpha* like nothing on the tongue again.

Behold

It is a face like a fog, see the gauze veil?
        It could be a girl whose features say
only paradise. She belongs to no one
        but blue light. The serpents
of Sumerian goddesses wind around her neck.
        You see

it is a woman with diamonds, white
        handkerchiefs fluttering like eyelids.
And the others, beloveds, made up
        like delicate mosaics. Floating
above them—light flooding from a distance,
        solace of the eyes.

On earth there is the wake, ear to ear,
        when we hear of the woman passing on—
eyes washed over in blindness, face washed
        clean of its weight. The survivors,
dark figures at the body, a gown for the journey.

In their gaze their mother imperceptibly
        disappears. They close their eyes
and remove their hands, so she rises.

You will fall in love again, perfuming your neck.
        And someone will bathe in it. The penniless
gather themselves in the company of bundles.
        Comfort, in the presence of, resting
in the gaze. As it will be, always,
        the atmosphere swirling around,
rolling over us with benevolent eyes.

A Picture of Us

Any two men looking love in the eye
Keep a short distance between themselves,
Shades drawn, overcoats on indoors,
As if under their shapelessness were all
That might somehow be wanted later on—
A lifetime's change of clothes or mind.

O fleshmate, soulmate, friend and focus,
My heart's first choice and last appeal,
Any lens is an hourglass the years sift
Slowly, swiftly through. May ours together
Fill a future that will have come out right,
Each of us, both of us, brought to light.

Levels of Intersection

Rain plows into the Willamette, rushes on.
A young man at a rest stop along I-5
Leans against his Ford Fairlane, smoking.
The sky is robin's egg blue, breaking through
Peaks and funnels of white clouds so immense
That giants might be hiding out in them,
Or throwing parties, or holding election rallies.
Maybe the man travels in a dream of love and money,
Driving to reunion or renewal.
And even if his heart is aching from the company
Of the radio, his journey is not forever,
His uneasiness a momentary weather.
Is that the memory of his mother's kiss
He puts away, the distant look in his father's eye?
Stubbing out his cigarette, does he see
Some welcome waiting for him north of here?

*

Now take away projection, the things we see
In others that are really just ourselves.
That leaves us with a young man in a Fairlane
Driving away under a clearing Oregon sky.
Who knows what he may be running from or
Driving to? Our intersection fixed the time, one day.
We saw him on his way somewhere, perhaps
To do somebody dirt, perhaps to repair.

William

Two nurses walk him
in the corridor
hold him up.
The young nurse dances,
makes him laugh.

At noon she is the one
who feeds him.
At medicine time
he clamps his mouth tight.
He is mostly docile
tries to talk, cries easily.

William's wife
feeds him supper
sits with him.
She has come every evening
and most mornings.
It is the necessary part
of her day.

Often his eyes focus
beyond her.
She wants to shake him.
Much of her life
she has been waiting.

from Unholy Data

"where the poet folds his green paper . . ."
—John Wieners

Laws were broken
There were no greener pastures
And now the quest to come clean

I regret the necessary substitution
I regret the trespass into secret places
I regret the turning away from Cordova

Poetry is not salvation
Damn references enchanted drifting it ain't Paradise
Rewritten lines with no-name characters

Royal blue, not enough
Dead men they don't cry out loud
Unending chain an eerie downward glide

Offshore the fabled ocean waits
Off the coast of Leucadia the props the props
And the fragments of a lighthouse.

Kayak
for Lawrence Fixel

We were exiles
back from Rome

to a home that was a house,
& a dead President.

Piles of traveling
& a foreign newspaper.

And there you were
on Laguna Street

a friend
who understood us.

How Space Travel Affects the Aging

WHAT THEIR BODIES KNOW

They're not used to it.
There's a lot their bodies have learned
to endure,
though,
facing a mirror or fingers—
yours or someone else's—
where a part of you is missing
or added.
Gravity
too little, too much
floating, free falling, pinned to the Earth
in magnetic boots going nowhere.
Thus patience in one place—
a sightseer unable to hike mysterious
mountains seen from a window,
take the old bike up those blue curves
or swim for miles in a foreign sea.
Sight: eyes will not be portholes long.
Perspective:
how space travel affects the aging
is a question that makes them laugh.
They know where they're going next.

HOW THE AGING AFFECT SPACE TRAVEL

No crew
No tests
Below
Just blue
Round globe
And you
Weightless

Satan Falls Among the Episcopalians
(a parable of the sixties)

Christ died for me on a Sunday
in June, 1965, not two years
after Jack Kennedy slumped into
Jackie's arms, her wailing to sirens
and the echo of something cracking
her consciousness of sunlight
in Dallas, blood flowing in and out
of the skull. So some believe Mary
Magdelene must have held him,
finally taken down like a sigh
or a ripe weighted fruit off
the tree of knowledge, the cross
of our sins, and whatever earthly
love she bore, so secret in her heart.
Love for his loins, forbidden in life
and now in her lap, curled in cloth
coming loose to the loose ropy
genitals he possessed so that
he might be a man. So I too was
becoming a man, knowing there is
America and there is the country
of the great white father and there
in the basement of our Episcopalian
Church, the puffy faced horn rimmed
seminarian whose name I've forgotten
debated fiercely with a thirteen year old
on the Church's knowledge of a just
war. Poor man. How earnestly
sweating he searched for answers,
eyes like a rabbit's rimmed with pink
and patience for the young punk
before him in his blue Sears suit.

How he glared at his pupil, how
his pupil glared back. And though
many questions mouthed themselves
in the teeth of this young interlocutor,
so many other questions never
crossed the boy's mind till years later—
Did it make a difference to this
priest in the making his inquisitor
was Japanese? Did Jackie know Jack
cheated with countless secretaries,
not to mention that tryst in L.A.
with a blonde goddess of Nembutal
and a few martinis? Did Christ
in the garden ever desire Magadelene?
(Or did he always know centurions
were waiting?) Why didn't the others
in my Sunday school class curse
my intransigent and ridiculous questioning
and point up at the clock every minute,
praying for the hour and service to be
done and time for juice and cookies
in the hall of the rectory? Why did
no one stop me from proclaiming
"I just can't see Christ down there
in the trenches" and prevent my falling
that moment into a No! that moved
from Christ to his Father to that war
against the gooks Jack kept escalating,
asking us all what can we do for our
country. Our president. Christ. Our Lord.

The Battle of Bruyeres (1944)

Perhaps there's nothing I can say, I who know nothing
of that village, its elms and willows and cottonwoods,
its fields where cows munched lazily even that day,
though perhaps they too paused and held their breath
at the boom of the howitzers or a sniper's ricochet
off the stone in the field. A stone too huge and ancient
and recalcitrant to move. A stone to be cursed or let be
as the plow cleaved on or the cow strayed to the creek.
Down in town there's a small spire of a chapel; beside it
a cemetery with graves centuries old, nearly illegible.
Perhaps the stones came from this field, companions
of the stone chipped now by a bullet and chipped again.
There's someone hiding behind the stone. A Nisei.
A soldier with the eyes of my uncle, a grape famer's boy.
All morning he's threaded his way through the trees,
and then the fields, his company prying out the Nazi's,
like threshers sweeping stalks before them, each man
holding the line, assured by some force beyond them,
the others will hold too. Nothing is broken here, just
go for broke. And he a katonk amid these Buddhaheads.
The sniper's somewhere down by the barn, the pen
of pigs, the stone farmhouse where a frightened family
huddles or has fled hours ago. And the man behind
the stone knows someone must make that dash across,
his thighs rustling against the wheat field, crows
breaking overhead, and the cow lowing by the creek,
stupidly safe and out of the battle, as he knows he's not.
And he thinks, his back strapped to the white stone,
that's how we're different, isn't it? A cow doesn't know.
A cow doesn't ask if this or the next moment ends it all.
That there's a choice between breaking for the barn
or breaking down here, weeping and weakening the line,
curling like a ball into the womb of the stone, so white
in the sunlight, blinding, as another bullet rips off a chunk.
And so he breathes and breathes again. Becoming stone.
And wonders at the start of the story. The Buddhist chant

his mother intoned each evening to the star at the window
where Heart Mountain rises with the towers in the dark.
Or the way the vines must be sheared and shaped, chosen
for their promise or snapped and stunted, for the good ones
to grow. How he hated that work, that sweat, his old man
muttering *hayaku, hayaku*, even in his silence, clipping
and crouching down the row. How the first grapes burst
upon his tongue, unlike the wine he never tasted as a boy.
Now he hears Izumi cry out, sees a green flak jacket
flattened on the field, like a rough brush stroke laid down
from a palette and by a brush not one of them understands
but only the words of their stocky sergeant Matsui barking,
Let's go, let's go. And the soldier leaps out, no longer stone.

Cross Section

Examination room #2 is about
to run dry of magazines. I've read
Sports Illustrated and *Vanity Fair*. I even
read *Money*, as if I had some.
Still no sign of the doctor. And, despite
the discrepancy between our
hourly rates, I calculate he now
owes me.

The only reading matter that remains
is a chart on the wall.
"Muscles of the Human Body"
was published in 1947. Not much
has changed since then.
It shows two views of the same stoic
figure, one facing, one turned away.
The fists are clenched to obligingly flex,
musculature exposed, vulnerable,
flayed.

I think of Michelangelo
elbow deep in cadavers seeking
structure, form, and line.
Then wonder who strung the cords
from forearms to the fingers? Who
braided taut hawsers of the thighs?
Who named the muscles as if they were
inner constellations, mythic heroes,
ancient emperors: Pectoralis Major,
Trapezius, Gluteus Maximus? I trace
the banded tendons crisscrossing
at knee and ankle the way a trainer
tapes an athlete, follow

tapering two-headed Gastrocnemius
to the heel, Achilles' weakness
and wound.

The doctor breezes through the door,
slaps x-rays on a lighted screen, and tells me
to remove my shirt. I stand
one side to the wall,
will deltoids, biceps, and triceps limp
as he examines my shoulder.
He gives me quick diagnosis, explains possible
surgical procedures, weighs treatments,
rehab, prognosis, then leaves me chilled
to dress.

From the window I watch uncharacteristic
rain spill down in bright sunshine,
look to find a rainbow. But what I see,
a body length away, is a tree
whose limbs all stretch skyward. Except
for one barren branch
that reaches down—four disconcertingly
elegant fingers, extended as if to grip the lawn,
rip away epidermal earth, peel it back
to reveal the raw and tangled cosmos
there beneath.

2 cats

it's real sweat & the voices are
armenian & the police car is still
north of fountain—parked. another
police car turns north on alexandria.
one block away. they're looking
for someone. & the bone has curved.
there's no turning back.

she had pasta primavera & a glass of
white wine. he had an 8oz new
york steak, medium rare. the wait-
ress talks him into having mashed
potatoes instead of french fries.
three tvs on, high in the corners,
no sound. the sound was cole porter.
silver lake, what do you expect?

the cats, in 100 degree weather, do
nothing slowly. the man sits in his
boxer shorts in front of the square
fan. & the heat is supposed to continue
through wednesday.

it's real silent except for the fan.
he can't think of anything but the
curving—it's like infinity.

Astonish Means "To Set the Teeth on Edge"

When I see the trumpet swans in winter preening themselves, I now know they do so to disperse an oil secreted by a neck gland: this keeps them warm in the most bitter weather. They seem to be making themselves comfortable, luxurious sadness, but they are actually insulating themselves. It's the same when we rant, on and on. We seem to be preening ourselves, but we are actually insulating ourselves. In the middle of a huge artificial pond swans can't feel all that threatened. Weak as us, though, and weakness hates weakness. It's nearly time to go home.

But clearly as this life the end never happens. What happens is that the door of every winter slams and shuts us inside. What happens is a huge room where we can put on our darkness and complain about our darkness. A crow strops its beak on a phone wire. Oak leaves chatter on lower branches, new contrails score the smudged ones. The seer is seen: so? Reciprocity can't stop the bulldozer that will plow up these trees by spring. Even the day-moon craps out—look at it up there, it's lost like a dog. The shiftings, hope-thin ice, fat drops from the icicles. And a crow: make no mistake, it cries.

As clearly as this life.

Smoke from My Mother's Mouth

I'd rub my eyes as I had in the family room
and in the family car and at the family restaurants—
decades of disbelief—
even as I'd rub my eyes she kept
reappearing inside smoke,
returning a look I swear almost too tender
to be happiness—
then whiplashed to some harangue of a eulogy—
some old story told on me—
and lit another one.
Vaporous innocence:
such as would break our heads—
but we couldn't talk or cry
out of each other's way.
And the birthday gifts opened to very little, as much as they could.
And the drive to see the goslings. . . .
those golden jots,
bobbing among their lighthouse-tall mothers and fathers,
their sentimental, sentimental
crap all over the golf greens—
"crap" was one of her pet words, her every sentence
crap was on its crossroads.
Geese in a child's sloppy v flew across the sky,
crying but using the cry
to travel on. And made their way,
and made her cry. I
hated tears, I hated the secreted tears.
I hated the second guessing,
how even before the presents opened, she had to say
these are lovely.
What were gifts to require her to cry?
The smoke never cried. . .
Never would. She could laugh,
and smoke
repeat what it had never said before.

Smoke I'd seen so many years
it seemed eternity had the blues.
Nor would smoke ever know the ravaged graces,
the gravities condensed to a sigh.
To drift away and where the wind knows not—
but it wasn't a heavy evil thing,
it was, like our loves,
taking leave. Like them it poured from our words.

Inaccessible Sea of Hillsborough River

This is a time when, of course
a river disarms every sound wave:
You were not the only child—

as if to die
without mentioning
death
were a sophomore
drama class.
And I can hear
the houselights
deny
everything is set
with diamonds
for the staring wave.

This is a time for those that never knew,
well of course, a young river always
looks for the sea.

Adolescents on Horseback

We rode the days we knew would always last—
Never spoke of the past. It meant nothing
To us lost in youth's eternal summer.
The high hill of sex? We climbed it, laughing,
In easy dark—felt our way by instinct.
The desert representing loss? We took
Tumbleweed tombstones for granted. Crossed
The river of no return? No problem.
We neither noticed nor knew its portent
As we galloped full-out through its current.
Motion was enough and we moved faster
To prove that we were living. What matter
If we never stopped, deeply thought
About anything? The future could wait,
For us to dismount. Then, like parents' traps,
It would spring, inevitably, questions:
Where had we been? What, by God, had we done?
To which we'd reply, innocent monks and nuns
Back from night-long vigil, "Nowhere. Nothing."

Barnsdall Park: The Frog is Sitting Backwards

I'm not there. The rain, you know—it would only be
wet grass, just staring at the park through my
car windows. And now it's 5:15 P.M.; the day evaporates.
The house will still be where it rose from Frank Lloyd Wright's
design. Stone hollyhocks. Some disrepair, of course.
Oh, God, this unreliability of stone, of grass, of every
day the way I tell myself this is my world, my stubbornness—
not everything will have to die.

Dear Andrea, I can't stop saying "grief" when you appear
along the edge, then I find tears, although
it's been eight months since you did die, like everything,
my longest friend, such health, until there wasn't anything but
cancer. How changed your body was from tall, large-footed, fast,
into medieval skeleton. The last gift was a black and silver pin
you gave to me at Christmas. Black: the new, hurt soul.
And silver: women's moon, the metal that has got to be kept up,
new-polished every time it's worn. The tarnish:
There's my fear, my rain-soaked feet,
even though I didn't make it to the park today.

Night's here. The patio outside my living room has shifted
from green fern to silhouette of plastic-covered chairs.
The rain is gone, but maybe not. Predicted for the weekend?
It's weather, always weather, bearing down or
letting up. I want the park. I want the hill it's on
that lifts above the city—that L.A. view, the European look
of houses scattered on more hills right under Griffith Park.
I'm struck again by how much city energy revives the raw,
unbearable collision of myself and Andrea's enormous absence.

And yet I've dreamed of her. She's well. I do believe
in dreams, and she has come to tell me she's just fine.
Death is not a judgment, or regret, or floating miserably in air.
It's—who can know? But something. Something like the
hollyhocks who stand erect and true against the weakened stone.
I can't stop grieving
but I can have faith in flowers rendered by an artist's hand
to represent the coming spring and summer. And yet I can't deny
that now it's even darker out there on the patio.

She's nothing but a box of ashes
covered up with dirt. She's nothing like a flower at all.

Barnsdall Park: The Delicate Glass of the Windows

Blue T-shirts saying "pilgrim" on the front. Down's syndrome kids,
round-faced, stumbling together, running on a flight of stairs.
("Eddie! Eddie! Eddie! Hey! Hey! Hey!") The sun picks out each
fat geranium along the gallery's wall—all shining here for
visitors from schools who cannot even know they have
a destination—even Eddie, center of attention. These pilgrims
flow in snakey inabilities, eventually complete their circle of
the park, gather for instructions, happily believe the teachers
who tell them that it's time to go. Go where?

Four quick days until my dead friend's birthday.
I want the afternoons we used to have when "pilgrim" meant
we'd be rewarded just because we made the trip, glad to trek
across the rough-earth field between her house and mine. A field
belonging to another park, Elysian—old, religious; and how
serious we were, in sun, in weeds grown to our ankles.
Our dialogues about This Life included evenings
at our neighbor Ann's, the Ann who once was married to a matador,
his body muscled, gifted, praised

until the bull that killed him came along.

Andrea and I across the field: we called each other by our living
names as sun jumped on our arms; we called the way they call
again, again for Eddie, leaping Eddie, happy Eddie, mortal Eddie.
Think about such afternoons as bold concertos all composed to
change—the shape we're born to and the illnesses we nurture
in ourselves. Make a civilized, warm-hearted bowing down, I
guess, even if blind luck is shit. And yet

I recognize the pungent eucalyptus smell—an herbal stringency—
that hits my nose as I pick up my notebook and my glasses, ready
to stop staring into God's blank cruelty. The odor comes as
medicine. I have my senses for right now, my body for a little
future, anyway. Am I thankful? I have never answered that.

Pilgrim in this foreign land, on foot.

What are you saying,

that the sky below
slips black and blue,

tree roots grip
to choke the pipes,

this open window
casts a shadow,

no one tells lies,
ice water rises

through clear air,
stars just aren't there,

old eggs float,
dog backs up God,

I never knew
one half of you.

Walking into the Dark Heart of Panama

Evening coming, young
    And afraid

I have wandered into
    The sudden dark

Of the jungle. Unsure of myself,
    Of which way to go

Bump into the wrong tree
    Black palm spines

Sweat in each puncture
    Mixes with blood,

One or two needles left
    Beneath the skin, stings

Remind me of who I am:
    Loveless, lonely, lost

Thirsting, remembering
    What I learned about survival

I cut beneath the spines to the heart
    Of the heart

Hold the juicy warm pulp
    To my face

All my fear and callowness
    Slip whispering away,

Beneath the jungle's canopy
      Into its erotic call

I dance to the castanets
      Of exotic insects, sing

With the nightbirds
      For all I'm worth

The Metaphysical Painters

What if, after the tulips' slow ecstasy,
the void? I see
through Magellanic clouds of veronica,
the amnesiac blankets of dandelions,
how the dark possibility
takes the lawn.

Only yesterday, last week—can't
put my finger on it—there was
a house, its eyes our eyes,
and we were in our houses traveling.
To shovel the past forward
gets us to snow's empery,
and the green swells, in turn,
to meet it.

Therefore, I
can't tell you of the provenance
of summer. The waves slaughter
themselves in rows, the ditch struggles.
They go down because it's nothing,
not the way I would take your shaping hand,
never to take up again
the mating of beauty to cruelty.

The Bird-man of Nogales

The Bird-man wasn't a bird
So much—he was a beaver, too,

With some horse and a flock of crows
Where the pupils of his eyes should have been.

He was a trapper in those years,
A prospector if he found a good rock.

Sometimes he was a sheep just grazing,
Just out there, an off-white

Part of a regular landscape,
Except up close.

He had gathered to himself through the years
Something of everything he knew,

A little bit of what he touched, his eyes
In their sudden blink

Catching, if just a molecule, a moment
From the glint of a sharp piece of quartz.

He was some parts animal, some parts
Shiny, and some parts so thin

They had no echo, or shadow, or taste.
He was dressed by his parts,

They took hold of him,
So a little of him snarled when he walked.

The shiny parts lit his way,
The human told him to eat.

He came down from the low mountains
Around town, fall of every year.

That was when he wavered, when Nature
Itself wavered, in its leaves,

In the air, in the brown.
He came to town for coffee,

For sugar, and to think.
He had a pony tail.

This was not a pony tail from a flashy decade,
This was not a pony tail for show or for fashion

It was more. The size and color of a forearm
Tattooed, with a mouth and two ears

In the right light.
It was a personal pony tail,

Something that lasted.
He had left it alone, uncombed

Ragged, pulled together but only a little,
Only as much as he could after years.

It matted itself and made grease;
It had a low order shine and a solid look,

The hairs more etched on than actually there.
From behind, the Bird-man was another thing,

A beaver at the top,
A split river at the blue jeans of his legs.

He drank his coffee slowly
And he stayed always about a month.

You could count on him.
This much of him was a season, too.

He didn't talk much, but he smiled
After awhile, after two weeks, or three.

It was a painful smile,
A little too much to the left.

Then somewhere in October every time
Some animal just came out of him.

It reached down with something like hands.
It pulled his pants a little higher,

Hard enough so we could see it.
Hard enough so that he had to get up.

He'd finish his coffee to the last,
But he felt it, too. He'd get up.

Then he would walk out, a little like a horse,
Until we couldn't see him.

Maybe he waved. Maybe
It was one of his large ears twitching.

He'd walk a line toward the hills, and go into them.
Into them, not over them.

Coffee in the Afternoon

It was afternoon tea, with tea foods spread out
Like in the books, except that it was coffee.

She made a tin pot of cowboy coffee, from memory,
That's what we used to call it, she said, *cowboy coffee.*

The grounds she pinched up in her hands, not a spoon,
And the fire on the stove she made from a match.

I sat with her and talked, but the talk was like the tea food,
A little of this and something from the other plate as well,

Always with a napkin and a thank-you. We sat and visited
And I watched her smoke cigarettes

Until the afternoon light was funny in the room,
And then we said our good-byes. The visit was liniment,

The way the tea was coffee, a confusion plain and nice,
A balm for the nerves of two people living in the world,

A balm in the tenor of its language, which spoke through our hands
In the small lifting of our cups and our cakes to our lips.

It was simplicity, and held only what it needed.
It was a gentle visit, and I did not see her again.

What Happened to Me

A boy rides a horse after school
On a warm day and clear
And on one day he does not hear
The call, one day does not come home.
The day is not less usual,
Not different from any other,
That particular day when now his mother
Cannot coolly bathe him, or comb
Or kiss his face, his hands, cannot
Fool this boy so easily about things.
The day is not different when he brings
Home nothing, though his hands are full.
On a warm day and clear
A boy rides a horse after school.
He is a small boy still
But the horse is big.
The world is there and this
Is its animal, and this,
His stepping off, is the getting on
The horse of the ground that will take him.

Ticket

This is the ticket
I failed to spend.
It is still in my pocket
at the fair's end.
It is not only
suffering or grief
or even boredom
of which we are
offered more than
enough.

Overcast

Outside it is raining white
Or did I read that somewhere
Where only white knows
anything this blank new year

A white season painted white
the color used too much
The sun rolled up into its socket
marbled over atrophied white

What does white mean
Bleached time Each day
more over than before
the past become more so

White is interest time pays
White pages are your passbook
The refrigerator hums white
The milk hums white too

The moon as well filmy at eleven
when the tv goes off and
a gauze passes over it
white going through a phase

Hard to imagine the moon
ever older or whiter than
it is already How one white
is not another white

How the ermine
opulence of clouds
is not the silent sleep
of winter snow

All white informs any white
most eloquent of silences thus
irresistible to those who hear
the intimations of nothing

The Gateman

While the rental car's radiator cooled on the shoulder
of the motorway—I was headed past Belfast
on the old M-2—a man appeared from the road-
blocked entrance to a factory annex across the yard
and offered to call ahead for me. The wind had dropped,
and the air, darkened by a recent shower of rain,
lent an odd, unearthly atmosphere to that small,
stooped-over shade of a man in mud boots and an anorak.
I said no thanks, I thought I'd wait, and as I waited
he lighted a roll-up and began to talk in the rough,
clipped accents of the Ulsterman. 'So you're a tourist,
are you, come to look around? Well, everyone's
a story here, that's for sure, and depending on which one's
telling it, it looks different told from different ways.

An outsider like yourself, you see, looking at
someone like me, no telling what he'd imagine.'
As he talked, his hands made quick parentheses
in air, as if bracketing the meanings of what he said,
then settled back, or lifted the cigarette to circle
an imaginary space before him. 'A nice enough fellow,
I suppose, the living example of your ordinary man,
perhaps a little too quick to know his place,
a little too settled on this or that or the other thing.
That's not so wrong now, is it? But from that
you're troubled to puzzle out how we've come
to figure in the world's eyes like a gang of
shadows railing each other in God's good name.'
He smiled once and nodded to me, though already

his mind was elsewhere. 'So where's the blame,
you're asking? Well I wouldn't be able to answer that,
but I will say this my friend. It's an enigma, I tell you,

the story of an enigma, an enigma inside an enigma.
And depending on which one's telling it, it looks different
told from different ways.' He trimmed his cigarette
and gathered himself around that thought, his eyes
fixed straight ahead. 'Still, I'm not the one to grumble.
It's not a bad job I've got, after all. I open the gates
and close the gates and I don't talk to anyone,
not a soul, and nobody bothers to talk to me.
Sometimes I feel like the man who's hired
to wait outside, watching for when Messiah comes—
the pay's not great, but it's steady work.'

                                         With that
he suddenly laughed out loud. With that he lighted
another cigarette and, turning up the collar of
his anorak, walked back across to the gatehouse
where he again took up his station. The sky
had darkened to a spattering of rain, the traffic
was swelling with the after-work rush, and like spirits
summoned back from the world, a thin, green-gray,
sulphurous haze lifted from the verges of the factory yard.
My friends were still an hour off, so re-starting
the engine I pulled back out onto the motorway,
and as I did he faded from sight in the rearview mirror.
And then the downpour broke, and like another
conversation building up in my head, the din
drowned out whatever thoughts I might've had just then.

Dem Bones

In the country I think of women's hips,
of a particular bowed angularity, the incredible harmoniousness
and universal clarity, the sense of justification in every corpuscle
a woman's body gives me, of the invulnerable breasts, the billowy thighs,
the moist central pavilion—and this is to say nothing
of the extraordinary character of women, the capacity
for sustained amiability, the credulous witticisms and unplanned
extended and moony exchanges, the taunts that shift to sweet
refusals to soft clamors that give way to the sexual mysteries...

It's like this in the country where I lie out in the fields at night,
supine in vegetable rows like something dropped from an airlift,
my free hand in a wet oracle, my tongue approaching, my gathered molecules
stiff as a hawk in a fight, hot as a bald spot
under a magnifying glass or a fire in a cotton warehouse...
And right over the tops of our bodies (as I'm picturing this)
winds sweep death like tufts of animal fur along the rows,
and once more from long-deserted lives comes forth the opportunity
to be of service, to express a connective garrulousness and
ingenuity that will, for a time, constitute and maintain
affection and a sense of the limitless possibilities of being alive,
love's like this...

Out of the wind a woman dives onto my body,
into my country soul, changing my city ways,
dispensing with the gravity of untenable monstrosities
(the misery of being human),
with the confused yet singular choruses of some hymn the "guide" sings
Love is form
and in a world without accidental occurrences, unduplicatible
and unusually investigated (Here's one more trip into the Unknown!)
just to the right of (and not to be confused with) the mistress Donne described
as smelling of pus and rotted cheese, lolling in her arms,

contorted and shuffled by grace (which follows mercy)
we will soon (as if wars were done) draw up our compact,
our truce and promise of mutual surrender, we who have compared
ourselves
to backdoor flagellants and bamboozled senior citizens
poking through the trash behind malls, (increasingly anonymous) lovers
going tediously on about sunsets and sumptuous Italian genres,
exhibiting a willingness (or tendency) to show
our appreciation for a phrase or a life well put...

I know I will succumb soon to the plunderings of time,
to the rifling of my pockets
and memory's slackened muttered reproaches,
I too will come on a former self stripping his bride
like a gift of folk art, dreaming even as I caress her
of women, maintaining a complimentary position among tomatoes
and green onions and other row crops,
yet, even as one who could never be forgiven, I am without confusion
as I approach the pleadings, the promises and simple facts,
like grandparents surprised en flagrante, the wet mouths
like tiny skulls crushed in the hand, unashamed, old lions
who glance up unconcerned from the carcass, going on
through the fall of man, passing this and continuing...

Dreams

I wake early from a dream of French poetry,
from the wellsprings of it, all rural in the dream:
a cripple in blue britches limps to a mossy well
contradicting himself as he comes.

Morning is a continuation of the dream
—the rusty, crippled hours, trees as if dipped in light syrup,
skaters coasting by, one man in black, drifting with arms folded...

I read over a few poems, make some changes in my mind,
dilute fabrications, push across a desert colored red
by sunset, bridge a gap in
the last scene between lovers
now too frail and bored to go on.

My mother was in my dream,
commenting on my looks and the way I dress.
You're too formal, she says.

      the early morning hours
extend generously into day

I read Italian poets; leftwing, outraged poets
from the Sixties (poets who are always leaving home),
and Pasolini,
distorted and enraged by lust,
a concentrate,
a man in a silver sidecar, the late poems
unburdening themselves of poetry

...and read a story
about a woman dreaming, who opens
fruit after fruit, orange pulp
and red squashed material
she doesn't understand, who watches her son
place speckled cowries on her sleeping body, a retarded boy...

each dream without relation to the day
catching its breath up ahead,

day a novelty
appearing at the exits of sleep,
a concession stand employee
who is actually your father.

My father once
in a cowboy suit outside school
performing poorly executed rope tricks.

At Home

I fell and it hurt. I fell
because I walked alone through a dark room
where the black dog slept.
I didn't turn on the light.
I could have asked for light but I walked
as though I were sure, hard
and quickly into darkness. Going
from one place to another, I fell
down across my big startled dog and it hurt!
Nothing could be more clear.
How long shall I stay humbled?
Bruised veins hostage my leg. Let my hand
reach out. The rest of me follow.
Let this dark room open its shape toward prayer.

Deer Season

On the next to last day of November
two men in different parts
of the forest took cold blessing
into their bones.

I stand at the door—
alone, sober in moonlight.
This door which was for later
now opens, into and out of the house.

Tansy Wormwood Sage

Who watered these greens
and greys? Who cut
and dried to feed her sheep
in winter? Who touched
the red bull's neck?
It doesn't matter, but I felt her
as the last herbs were cut today.
The grey clapboard house
warmed with October's sun.
It doesn't matter,
but I stood there
one moment more exact than ever
returning home.

Again

When the gifts have all been opened,
the turkey eaten and the carcass
stripped for soup, when the sons
have been put on planes and the empty
wine and whiskey bottles trashed
and the dead pine peeled of lights
and dragged to the curb, and when all
the football games have been lost or won,
and all the rabbits shot,
what remains? What weariness walks
under a thin moon? What birth
has promised us what death and how soon?
And we wonder, and we shame, and go
down again on our knees—

Symmetry

Consider a lopsided mushroom
leaning toward straight
or a dwarf straining toward tall
or an ice cream cone: lick/twirl
lick/twirl till a sharp peak
rises in the middle.

Consider feet, their two shoes,
and eyes, their two stares,
and lips, their two flaps.
And consider their hopes:
the glass eye, the sixth finger
chopped off, the plastic legs
on roller skates.

Somewhere something wants me crooked.
I don't know who or what or why,
but I do know I must part my hair
straight down the middle.

Winter Hits
after Li Ho

Crows in the windy alley flick the heart: a gladness.
Bound under ice, the city's arrested—

take a seat in the middle of the street and meditate.
So who loves this January weather? The consolation

of shadow, indigo veins of snow on a pitched
roof. And crows, their voices wrecked—cured,

too late, from scotch and cigarettes—talking trash
to some young girl who won't be rushed,

a rookie kid just learning to weave, laying down
threads the crows steal for her from the low-cut sun.

Each day she weaves in one more minute, more minute
of light for those bonnie hoodlums, who do not

fly south, who are thieving—but not mutinous—
and whose voices, cracked by a thousand blizzards,

do not forsake her.

Revisiting Ozymandias

On looking at a photo of a sculpture, *The Last Supper* by A. Szukalski,
imbedded in the shifting isolation of the Nevada desert

Each figure faces a different direction
like leaves keyed to the gifts of God's last light; it is
the illusion of center that will move even sunflowers
against force fields of personal desire.
What does it mean to be astonished
by El Greco's knowledge of agony, the symmetry
of sitar music drawing the mind toward madness
or that goofy smile on the faces of saints?
If I met perfection in the desert,
I'd expect it to be a wistful Ozymandias
on the way to total disintegration,
but I'd recognize it, and its imprint, and its echo, and its argument.

At the last supper, someone must have told a joke,
just to break the tension, and someone else
insisted on correctness. Each job was chosen,
each assigned, each essential. Knowing this,
I don't empty my heart in despair. For this picture
has been repeated over and over, thirteen ghosts,
silver shrouds, what the artist must give over to entropy
and what the poet grabs and hides inside
her mouth. Be grateful it is white as a new mind,
moored to the desert floor. If it is obscured
by dust storms or an impatient foot on the gas,
you can always rely on the photograph
left on the inner eye of the bug in the rock
that you carry, on the shadow
left by candlelight on the half-moon of your nail.

Speculations

If I could only write one word
It would be salt. I don't know why.
Not for memory—for the sea
they tell us we come from.
Not for the way our bodies move
exchanging solutions
we've called love.
Perhaps because salt's almost bitter
yet necessary—nearly salvation—
the taste of work and pain.
Because put on melons, it makes sweet
more sweet. Because I would bring salt
to Dad and Granddad when they drank beer
but once brought garlic salt instead—
that joke we always laughed about.
Because salt's in the desert
where prophets go—because
it stays nailed in the earth
when water's gone.
Or more likely because salt
is short, simple, the rock
inside us. A place to start.

Custodian
for charlie fanning

I ran the shovel along the street,
a razor path through the sidewalk's face,
snowy lather parting for me, for my father,
our feet crunching in the city night.

We grabbed the garbage cans from school
and church and dragged them up the iron
stairs. I lugged burlap bags stuffed
with bingo cards, light as cream puffs.

We swept the auditorium with green sawdust
from huge drums. We hammered and drilled
in his workshop, where tools hung on pegboard,
their images silhouetted behind them

For instant identification and placement.
Once he sawed his index finger in half
on the power saw in a moment of inattention
in a life otherwise constructed of skill and care.

Once a year the Monsignor made him climb inside
the giant boiler and clean it out
with enormous pipe cleaners till he was black
with soot that took days to wash off.

Sonny boy, he called me, and laddie buck.
He always said just do your best.
All of us loved to watch him fall asleep
on the couch, *Daily News* over his face,

snores filling the apartment
with the music of rest well deserved.
His finger took years to heal enough
for him to play again but a black scar

ran down its center. He'd give me a rub
with his unshaven face, rough as sandpaper.
He'd pretend he didn't know me, scrubbed from
the tub, the lovely lie delighting me every time.

Audacity

Every Catholic in New York cringed
at the sight of him. Holy-mary
piety, androgynous, nunlike demeanor,
fat cherubic face only made his warlike
politics and egomania seem more intense,
scarier. Inside we all knew he was mean
and vain. Kids from every parish cut down
in Vietnam while Spellman waltzed with
J. Edgar Hoover and built monuments to himself.

Spellman Hall at my college,
other Spellman halls at other schools.
A little archipelago of namesakes.
Even children mocked his audacity.

When Cardinal Spellman High School opened,
in a crummy part of the Bronx in a temporary,
ugly, squat building, no one wanted to go.
But the archdiocese offered incentives
to tempt the flock (an easy ride,
low tuition) and soon enrollment surged.

Even my father, school custodian
and good Catholic, had no use for him.
The Cardinal set up a bogus pension plan
leaving those who had labored a lifetime
for the church with nothing at the end
but a handshake and a shove out the door.
You didn't retire under Spellman.
You worked till you died poor.

Poem for My Son

Each time you connected I strode among junipers
And ankle-twisting stumpholes to where it seemed the ball had landed.
You waited and gave occasional directions:
"In front of the apple tree. To the right of the boulder, I think."
Before each pitch arrived your boy's body grew taut.
You were like a green snake—lithe, patient, concentrated.

In spring, the hardball's plummet
Ended in a soggy plop. Grounders skidded rather than bounced.
In summer there were wild strawberries—
The tiniest winces of fruit-sugar.
We lolled in the modest northern heat and watched
The grasshoppers inherit the earth.

Sometimes while throwing the ball I critiqued
Your swing: "The most difficult of physical feats,
Hitting a baseball." Or I chattered: "The game was not invented
In America but evolved like a—"
You were correct to interrupt. Pleasure wanted
The uncanny knack of concentration: not bearing down too hard
Nor assuming valiant strength would right all flaws.

You rarely flailed in vain. Eventually, you could have
Started for any school team, but we lived far away
From the practiced accuracy of diamonds.
Whatever was to be learned, in all its amplitude,
Had to be done there, on a sloping, runneled field.

The God of Wine

Dionysus is big enough to get up
onto the kitchen counter now. Five months old
and cleaning the sink with his tongue.
He has already tasted last night's lasagna
on unwashed plates, salt sweat of human hands
from a stack of quarters for laundry,
and sunlight's dust settled onto the counter.
But it will be night before he makes his way
to the cluster of Cabernet bottles,
holds the first neck in both paws
and stretches to taste the blood of grapes.
Will he hold the mouth of that bottle
longer than he holds my finger
in his own small mouth?
He'll never know how it feels
to pull the last drops from a glass
and let them slide down your throat
before you abandon the kitchen
for the lover waiting in the next room,
or how easy it is
to let wine spare the tongue its trouble,
to be human and silent in doubt.

Reviews

The Language of Grief

Ghost Volcano. Sandra M. Gilbert. New York, NY: Norton, 1995. III pp. $II paper.

It is May 1999 and I, like most Americans, am sated with images of the recent school shootings in Colorado—the grainy traces of teenagers fleeing for their lives, the Town Hall interviews with Ted Koppel, the ponderous self-importance of round-the-clock cable TV coverage. Beneath the questions of violence, culpability, complicity, and intent lies a deeper issue that troubles late 20th century Americans as much as do our apparently murderous tendencies: that is, how do we mourn the dead? Armies of well-educated grief counselors descended on that bland Denver suburb, and in a familiar national spectacle we were treated once again to the contemporary language of bereavement, while journalists intoned—indeed promised—that "closure" would be ours if we just talked things through, held hands, lit candles, wore ribbons, and wrote poems on the glistening white coffins.

Faced with the immeasurable ordinary catastrophe of death, how do any of us find words adequate to the experience? Poet Sandra M. Gilbert had this question thrust upon her in 1991, when her husband of 30 years died unexpectedly after surgery. The fruit of this terrifying experience is *Ghost Volcano*, a collection of several dozen lyrical poems charting Gilbert's chronology of grief and four elegiac poems that meditate on violence, mortality, history, and mutability. This book is a formidable achievement from one of the finest American poets writing today. Gilbert shows us that loss now demands a radically different formal response, as if our fractured post-industrial moment can no longer find solace in the pastoral elegy or threnody that served writers from Theocritus to W. H. Auden. The poems are stripped, honed, yet stunning in their use of unorthodox detail matched by rich philosophical inquiry. Meticulously sculpted from the pain of loss, *Ghost Volcano* contains a fully-formed and absolutely true world.

Written at the same time Gilbert recounted her husband's death in a book entitled *Wrongful Death: A Medical Tragedy* (Norton 1995), the poems of Ghost Volcano form the antiphon to that narrative, allowing Gilbert to discover the pitch and heft, depth and resonance of her grief. This collection is Gilbert's fifth and bears the stamp of her style. She is a poet who has read deeply and possesses an unerring ear for rhythm, an iconoclastic eye, a keen sense of our cultural moment, and an extraordinary sensitivity to the beauty of language. Gilbert knows intuitively that mundane personal details, such as the dead husband's carefully-noted burial garments of blue tweed sport coat and Liberty of London tie, are capable of amplifying the universal appeal of these poems. Indeed, the collection weaves a well-wrought garment of words, which functions as the burial shroud, the widow's shawl, and the tablecloth at the mourning feast that comprise our shared mortality.

The Widow's Walk Lyrics are individually dated and cover a period of roughly three years, beginning eight months after the death of Gilbert's husband. The poems were composed in a wide range of places, in Europe, Mexico, and across America. Their contexts are as varied as the emotions they register. The change of seasons in New York State, for instance, commences the lyric sequence with a bitter admission: "I always hated Halloween,/ the fat dead pumpkin with its silly mask/ of life, the kids pretending to be ghosts,/ the mockery of skeletons" ("October 26, 1991, Outside Saratoga Springs"). In the poems that follow, Gilbert contemplates her solitude, her disbelief, her rage, wryly alluding to the contemporary language of self-help which, in "December 21, 1991: Berkeley Solstice," offers a hollow consolation that echoes (intentionally?) Spielberg and "Poltergeist:"

> ...that famous tube of light
> through which the near dead pass into—
> into what they cannot know.
>
> "The light is kind," says my grief book.
> "The light is good. Those who have seen this light
> don't fear it."

Some poems present a perfectly anesthetized speaker who is alert, nonetheless, to acute surrounding details, as in "January 30, 1992: On the Beach as Santa Barbara," which juxtaposes the offshore "oil rigs, the yachts, the trawlers" that float "becalmed on some bizarre gray tissue/ that blurs in a sullen sky" with the speaker's memories of "the ice-white light of the O.R." A later poem, "May 3, 1992: On the Surface," strikes me as a brilliant exercise in controlled hysteria. The poem is glazed with a kind of lunatic normalcy, and the speaker in short, almost asthmatic bursts gives her dead husband an update on current events:

...on the surface, certainly,
the oaks are pollinating, sexual and yellow,

yellow-green,
and the kids are fine, too, really,

even if down there this new
warmth hasn't trickled through

to you,
and it's so dull, I know,

and I suspect,
nothing touches what's inside the silent

boxes, nothing creeps into the heaviness
that covers all of you

except the bulbs, the dreadful bulbs exploding
everywhere and rising

toward the surface
through this season's placid grass.

I fully expected to see the rough outlines of Kubler-Ross's well-known grief stages in these lyrics, which take their name from the 12th poem in the sequence ("June 15, 1992: Widow's Walk, Harpswell, Maine"). Yet even though the collection's last verse tentatively offers the possibility of "bitter joy," the Widow's Walk poems nonetheless serve as a rebuke to the populist grief industry's faith that the living will "get over" the dead, in successful and successive steps. Instead, denial, rage, bargaining, and disbelief ricochet back and forth, stubbornly failing to line up in the neat chronological pattern that might be called a progression. Nowhere is this more evident than in the extraordinary "March 14, 1993: Berkeley: Trying Not to Think of a White Bear." Here the speaker weighs the philosophical advice of well-meaning friends, who gently suggest that her obsession with her dead husband can be solved by abstraction. But like the young Tolstoy in the poem's epigram, who would be forgiven an infraction if, for five minutes, he could not think of a white bear, so too the speaker finds that the white bear in *her* consciousness is not so easily dismissed:

...I tried. Five more seconds.
This time I could see her claws:
steely hooks, I thought,
the size of picture hangers,

and she was twice my height, and as she moved
I noted lice or fleas, jumpy commas,
troubling her pelt so that the fine hairs
flipped and flicked.

In a moment of desperate and triumphant insight, the speaker concludes, "I can't not think of a white bear/ the way I can't not think of you."

This admission is consistent with *Ghost Volcano's* implicit eagerness to ask impertinent questions about our relationship to death and grief: What do we hope to accomplish by writing about the dead? Do we seek to make the word flesh because of arrogance or for therapeutic ends? How do we interpret our ventriloquised conversations with the deceased—are these talks pathological, even narcissistic? How, moreover, can we stop thinking about the White Bear when we live in an age that is embarrassed by prolonged grief and demands closure, resolution? (In fact, one might also ask whether lengthy bereavement has surpassed sex and money as our modern taboo subject). Gilbert recognizes her role as one who puts the words of the living into the mouth of the dead, and she questions her motives, as in "September 10, 1992: Picking Wildflowers in New Hampshire":

You'd love, I know, the cottages in the pines...

                    and love, I think, the sudden
furtive spears of goldenrod...

You'd love! I hate the phrase, I hate that bleak
subjunctive, never ending, always postulating
the impossible.
                What *would* you love, what *can* I love,
in the empty meadow, the unpeopled houses?

And again, in "Spring Equinox, 1993: Puerto Vallarta 7 Playa de Los Muertos," Gilbert meditates on the universal impulse to reanimate the dead. Here she imagines "the dead are bathing, complacent" but forgetful that "it's hard to walk without the drag of the body,/ to swim/ without the flesh that rises on the curve/ of every wave...." The poem continues:

> That's why
> they need us, *you* need *me*:
> to walk, to wish.

The poem's concluding benediction is as near to closure as this collection is likely to offer:

> I send you forth—you deeply burning
> in yourself like a floating candle,
> you musing and lit with your own past
>
> I send you like a hieroglyph, or a letter
> to God, across the shining gulf,
> toward the unimaginable ice cliffs
> south of the south.

In the four formal elegiac poems that round out *Ghost Volcano* ("Kissing the Bread," "Notes on Masada," "Water Music," "Calla Lilies") Gilbert explores grief in historical, even depersonalized terms, shifting the collection's focus from raw subjectivity to the polished granite of a universal vision. *The Princeton Encyclopedia of Poetry and Poetics* (1974) defines the elegy as "a lyric, usually formal in tone and diction, suggested either by the death of an actual person or by the poet's contemplation of the tragic aspects of life. In either case, the emotion, originally expressed as a lament, finds consolation in the contemplation of some permanent principle." Given that we live in a deconstructed, postmodern world where absolute, "permanent" principles have been unmasked as either harmless fictions or hegemonic plots, Gilbert's poems struggle to uncover Platonic certitudes (beyond the fact of death itself) but reveal instead only decline, decay, transformation, transliteration in fact, a Heraclitean fire of mutability. Even the glorious calla lilies that "sway and bow in the Easter breeze" have "forgotten the wrists and ribs of the dead/ from whose pallets they have risen." These delicate concluding lines from "Calla Lilies" celebrate the beauty of life's relentless impulse for renewal. At the same time, however, they unmask that renewal's dependence on a kind of collective amnesia a forgetting made paradoxically impossible by the speaker drawing our attention to the act of forgetting.

The fragility of the flesh is further developed in "Kissing the Bread," which refers to the Sicilian custom of kissing stale bread before throwing it away. Bread's multiple meanings as body of Christ and staff of life serve Gilbert well. The speaker is both a baffled eight-year old and an adult, puzzling over this ritual, working through its possible significance in Christian and pagan terms. It suggests the transience of the flesh ("Kissing the bread was kissing/ the carrion that was the body/ of every body..."). Most important, the kiss enacts a ceremonial rehearsal of all the losses to come, the bread metonymically suggesting the human form:

> ...my mother's kiss
> was humble, the mortified
> kiss of guilt—*I can use you*
> *no longer*—and the kiss
> of dread: *what will I do, challah,*
> *pumpernickel, rye, baguette, sweet white,*
> *thick black, when you*
> *are gone?*

"Notes on Masada" is a powerful meditation on faith in the context of one of Judaism's most hallowed monuments, the site at Masada where more than 900 faithful killed themselves rather than surrender to the Romans. As a non-Jew married to a Jew, the speaker broods uneasily over her place in this spectacle. Is she the outsider, the onlooker, the one whom the Jewish zealots would spare? As the outsider, is she the potential killer? As a Christian who may have remote and unidentified Jewish relatives, is she a member of the tribe who is killed? Or is she perhaps one of two remarkable women who escaped—women who are described in the poem's epigraph from *The Jewish War* as being "in intelligence and education superior to most women"? The questions are rhetorical, unanswerable, resonating with the guilt of the survivor, the fear of death, and the secret murderous impulse the speaker fears in her own breast. Haunted by her tepid faith, she nonetheless lights a candle at her husband's urging ("I crossed myself, spurious, and 'prayed.'/ 'Mass psychosis,' I complained, hovering/ next to Israeli honeysuckle, breathing hyssop and cinnamon..."). "Notes on Masada" reads like a passion play, its slow, deliberate movements suggesting the stations of the cross. But its thirteen parts fall one short of that Christian ritual. I have to believe, however, that this deviation is deliberate; the misstep is, after all, in step with the speaker's halting progress through the "vicious blue" of Masada's alien landscape.

Finally, "Water Music's" nine sequences serve as the book's philosophical heart. Here the themes of transformation, mutability, and the limits of the corporeal are developed through the image of water: briny saltwater, sweet grape juice water, translucent veined cabbage leaf water, mineralized scum of water, ice-cube tray corralled water, landscape tables of water, lakes of water, rain. Humanity flickers shadowily, fitfully in these verses a "venerable" head is haloed by molecules of water; a drowsy reader is wakened by a torrent of rain. Indeed, the detachment of the voice its orphic echoes recalls the tone of another great elegiac work, Virginia Woolf's powerful "Time Passes" section in *To the Lighthouse*. The language of these poems is dreamy, fluid, almost incantatory, as if Gilbert were mimicking the low even pulse of the blood, reminding us that our solid bodies are four-fifths liquid. Listen, for example, to these verses from part I, "The Nature of Water":

First, the clarity, those
molecules you go through and through,
and through you they go

in the long sift of blood.
And the shine goes through
as if something—you?—believes

in color, something stipulates
now blue, now what's called
green or black....

Other sections reveal a sly wit, as in "The Ice Cubes," which are described as prisoners in iron jail cells yearning for transformation: "*Let us go/ out of shape,* the cubes demand,/ out of exquisite/ ache, out of Plato's arrogant/ mind, out of// humiliating Euclid." And the final section, entitled "Rain" places chaos just at the edge of consciousness, as if the tumultuous fact of our watery selves must be kept from us:

And you who nod beside the reading lamp,
seeing in a drowned half-sleep
only the pink of your fingers
as they cling to the edges of this page,

have you heard that seething from the sky?
By the time you wake,

shake yourself,
and rise to close the blinds,

it is over and it is calm, calm
and over.

"Water Music" is an act of sheer poetic bravado. It is illegible as elegy only if we limit ourselves to meditations on mutability anchored in the Absolute. But Gilbert knows that the formality of grief and the unyielding mountain range of death's finality must yield to a vision of the fluid, the infinite.

This collection begins with an icy image of the husband's face staring up from the mouth of Mount Rainier: *"sometimes you see it / sometimes you don't."* When, nearly three years later, Gilbert acknowledges in "February 14, 1994: At the Point Reyes Lighthouse" that "you are still stopped dead" she is both at the same place and paradoxically beyond it, touched now by the plumes of spray from migratory whales: "The film of their breathing/ flaps banners of bitter/ joy in the salty wind." To be sure *Ghost Volcano* shows that we will be changed by mourning even as the object of our loss is likewise changed; and our human response will of necessity demand pulling down the blinds on the storm roaring outside. But I for one am grateful to have these wise, courageous and insightful poems, if only because they offer me a believable way to confront the horror of loss.

Review by Joseph Duemer

Calls and Responses: An *Elegy* of Larry Levis

Elegy. Larry Levis (Forward by Philip Levine). Pittsburgh, PA: University of Pittsburgh Press, 1997. 85 pp. $12.95 paper.

First call: When I was a young man I loved the early, smartaleck Larry Levis; now that I am older, I am taken by the more contemplative poems Levis wrote just before his death from a heart attack at fifty. Different architectures for different times in a life. When I was young I lived in rented rooms and only cared about the surfaces of the walls, to which I might tack pictures; now I live in my own house and I am interested in the way it sits on the earth, in the way its wires and pipes behave (and misbehave) and when I drive a nail into a wall I know the painting I will hang there is a hedge against death. Perhaps that sounds overly dramatic, but Levis has put me in mind of Rilke—how could he not?—and Rilke is fond of dramatic locutions. I also take for Rilke's elegies the idea that part of being a grownup in this world is being aware that the angel of death is always there hovering just off your left shoulder, dragging its wing in the dust. If you are a lucky poet, the angel may from time to time whisper wisdom into your left ear. Levis, I think was a lucky poet. Even in his earliest work, his sense of mortality kept his eye sharp and his wit keen.

Second call: The best American poetry of the last twenty to thirty years has expended its energies in developing sufficient escape velocity to break free of the gravitational pull of the "organic" lyric. The career of Larry Levis, who died in his fiftieth year in 1996, coincides with this arc, or spiral, away from lyric unity. Different groups and schools of American poets have moved away from the romantic / organic lyric during this period, of course—in this Levis is not unique. Only the self-proclaimed New Formalists have staunchly held out for the lyric detached from history—all the while, it must be noted, proclaiming their revolutionary intentions. Such is often the case with reactionaries. While not unique in its movement, then, Levis' career presents the reader with a narrative of personal development and recognition. If Robert Lowell, in the generation preceding Levis, seems to have moved from mature adult to charming if needy child, Levis became in his last two books fully poetically adult.

Third call: Let me try again. American poetry in the last quarter of the twentieth century has been forced by history to negotiate the divorce from forms deeply loved & understood since the Romanticism of the nineteenth century. Levis, on the evidence of his earlier work was fully conversant with romantic conventions, and if he never wrote sonnets, he fully explored the genre of the Coleridgian conversation poem and the Wordsworthian meditation, though he often undercut the reader's expectation with wit, non-sequiter, or deep-image absurdity. Deeply romantic, Levis learned, too, from James Wright and John Berryman, especially the techniques for handling extreme emotions in controlled language. (Levis' feel for the absurd detail is another way in which he subverts lyric expectation.) Levis' final three books form an arc of increasing discontent with traditional means. In *Winter Stars* the stanzas remain regular and there is a loose iambic pulse beneath the free-verse lines; in *The Widening Spell of Leaves*, though, Levis begins to tease apart both line and poetic structure in search of a wider poetic way of spelling; that poetic process is fully developed in *Elegy*. It is difficult to know whether, had he lived, Levis' poetry would have unraveled into silence or wandered in the back streets of the garrulous. Probably, given the anarchistic and empiricist ethic revealed by many of the later poems, he would have found new ways of writing. The early poems in *Elegy*— credit David St. John's editing—recapitulate the manner and technique of earlier books, but by the second section the reader is in new territory, plunged beneath the veil of an icy waterfall of language.

Thesis: Fever and chills; empiricism and hallucination; silence in the face of death; redemptive beauty.

First response: Rilke, in *Malte Laurids Brigge*, has his central character say, "Who cares anything today for a finely finished death? No one. Even the rich, who could after all afford this luxury of dying in full detail, are beginning to be careless and indifferent; the wish to have a death of one's own is growing ever rarer." Brigge has been walking past the Hotel Dieu in Paris, an institution on its way, in Rilke's time, to becoming a modern, industrial style hospital. Brigge waxes quite witty on the modern way of dying. It is a wit that seeks to puncture the polite balloons of language we raise as we pass along the streets pretending we are not dying. What staggers the reader about the poems in this last book by Larry Levis is that it seems so filled with consciousness of personal mortality—the individual human being swallowed up by history. For Levis, history has become God. Levis presents us with Rilkian portraits. One of the qualities Levis shares with Rilke is an ability to speak in his poems with what I'd like to call a "theological irony," that is, an irony that also means to be taken seriously, even literally. When God cracks a joke, one had best listen carefully. Both Rilke and Levis aspire to speak in a voice that is, finally, scriptural and deeply personal. God's great joke, of course, is his non-existence, his replacement in this century by history. This is a profoundly different impulse from that of a poet like Mark Jarman, who, in his recent "Holy Sonnets" aspires only to speak to God and about God.

Second response: Since I have been reluctant to write a panegyric here, though that is what I originally expected of myself, I have thought to ask the heretical question: Who might not like this book? Who might not approve its procedures? A critic of formalist or New Formalist bent would likely fault Levis for laxness, especially in the construction of his lines and the meandering structures he employs. And such a critic would be right—Levis was out to get the lyric. But the schools of post modernism would fault him, too, for concern with the creation of a personal voice. Voice is one thing post-modernists hate above all else, for the post-modern poem is written not spoken. Speaking, true, is a fiction on the printed page, but so is the myth of objectivity and the linguistically "pure" poetries favored by the avant garde. Larry Levis, in *Elegy*, is stuck between the demands of the various schools. A realist and empiricist, he moves subjectively toward song, song in a way of gesturing toward experience and toward the world. These poems freely admit the impossibility of poetry and convince the reader of its absolute necessity.

Third response: In any event, it is hard for a reviewer to know what to say in the presence of such eloquence, especially when the poems are surrounded by the silence of Levis' now-completed life. The poems themselves—beyond the accident of an unexpected death—seem bathed in silence. As long as some of these poems are, they evince an acute awareness of Wittgenstein's insight that "what we cannot speak about, we must pass over in silence." That is the early Wittgenstein; the later one concluded that, at best, we might point to such things as love, loss, joy, or beauty. Might indicate them with a sentence. So it is a discursive silence Levis employs in *Elegy*. That must be why so many of them are so long and end so inconclusively. That must be why, like music, a theme is developed, then abandoned, then picked up again later. If the elegy is usually a lyric, this book violates the generalization; for Levis as for Donne, the elegy is meditative and—in the case of Levis—symphonic is structure. (But even the symphony exfoliates in *Elegy*, for the structures remind one far more of Mahler than of Haydn.) This difference points to a paradox in our usage: *elegy* can mean a poem for the dead, or a meditation, where that word is understood to convey both the idea of inner thought and the background of mortality against which all thought transpires.

Note: "What are the grievous things? What the gracious?" Rilke's Notebooks deny the need for proofs of God's existence, not because they are impossible but because they impose such a heavy responsibility upon those who accept them. Better to believe or not without proofs and logical quibbles. In Elegy, the "gracious things" are represented by horses. Up to this point I have quite intentionally not quoted any lines of poetry in this review—this is a book that must be taken whole and that cannot be understood or even approached through quotation. In conclusion, though, this:

> The brow of a horse in that moment when
> The horse is drinking water so deeply from a trough
> It seems to inhale the water, is holy.

I refuse to explain.

Review by Jeanne Girolo-Hoffman

Dislocation, Tradition and Self in Carolyn Kizer's *Harping On*

Harping On—Poems 1985-1995. Carolyn Kizer. Port Townsend, WA: Copper Canyon Press, 1996. 70 pp. $12.00 paper.

In the most compelling modernist poetry, dislocations of time and space maneuver us to engage the strange, the sense of other, a world even more complex than its tempestuous surface suggests. As rich in form as in meaning, it engages most when it ratifies our felt need for story. In Carolyn Kizer's new book, *Harping On*, everything is here: the finely detailed particulars of a passionately lived life; an intellectual and generously ironic *joie de vivre*; deep convictions in the context of a sweeping, idiosyncratic sense of history and poetic tradition; constant surprise; and most importantly, the recurrent delights of her formally controlled narrative verse.

In a time when all manner of boundaries are blurring, Kizer's work consistently rewards with intricately realized distinctions that emerge through her inventive braiding of structure and narrative. Kizer continues to experiment with forms. And it is within her captivating poetic voices—struggling, enraged, rapturous, funny, elegant, compassionate—where we discover a world more astonishing in its contemporary shape, and a past richer and dearer for her masterful enactments. Subjects range over a multitude of landscapes: international, geographical, artistic, political, historical and cultural, reflecting this poet's varied, distinguished career. But despite Kizer's great erudition and breadth of experience, her poems refuse to abandon the legacy of loved ones as central themes.

Of the twenty-nine poems in *Harping On*, written between 1985 and 1995, perhaps the soaring four-page dramatic narrative "Gerda" best illustrates Kizer's protean talent. Beginning with an epigraph from an old Swedish children's prayer, memory and history drive the story, while dream and fairy tale help manifest the poem's multiple perspectives:

> Down the long curving walk you trudge to the street,
> Stoop-shouldered in defeat, a cardboard suitcase
> In each hand. Gerda, don't leave! the child cries
> From the porch, waving and weeping; her stony mother
> Speaks again of the raise in salary

Denied. Gerda demands ten dollars more
Than the twenty-five a month she has been paid
To sew, cook, keep house, dress and undress the child,
Bathe the child with the rough scaly hands
She cleans in Clorox; sing to the child
In Swedish, teach her to pray, to count her toes
In Swedish. Forty years on the child still knows how

From the beginning, rhythmic techniques—such as recurrent guttural "r" sounds, the measured cadence of Scandinavian speech, steady repetition of Gerda's name clothed in lineaments of fairy tale ("Blind Gerda gropes for her steel-rimmed spectacles," "the dress/ Gerda smocked at night while the household slept"), repeated reference to "the child"—all result in a Bergmanesque amalgam of nostalgia, fear and fantasy. The cumulative effect is to render the poem's operatic flow, as past and present merge:

She came to us. Twenty-five dollars a month
To sew a quilt for the child, covered with fabulous
Animals feather-stitched in blue and white;
Now after fifty years it hangs on the wall
Of the child's grandchild, in a Chicago house.
Then, when the child awoke, addled and drunk with nightmare,
She dragged the quilt from her cot,
Stumbled sniffling into Gerda's room,
To be taken back into her bed, soothed back to sleep
By the rough, antiseptic hands.

Vivid surface details thicken with ever-broader strokes until at midpoint when the child's confusions are tautly encased:

Thirty years on, her father will remark,
"Your mother was jealous
So we let her go. Of course I could have raised her wages,
Gerda ran the house!" The child's throat fills with bile

In verse seven, the child's sick spirit transforms into the child's sick body, a new form of desperation:

The child's eighth year, like Gerda, disappeared.
Hazy recall of illness:
Asthma, the wheeze, the struggle for breath,
And the louder rhythmic wheeze of oxygen ...

Languorous images slow recollection: "the pallid joys of recovery/ Jello and milk, ice cream three times a day . . ./ Dreamily sucking a spoonful of melting vanilla:/ Only these splinters of a vanished year." Then action speeds with a chilling interior climax, striking notes both of Rimbaud and Poe:

It must have been then that the ice-house dream began,
Her first and last recurring dream:
The child stands in a little room of ice;
Outside a song begins, impossibly nostalgic,
Played on a concertina or harmonium.
As the dream goes on
Slowly, slowly the walls move in, the ceiling presses down
Till she is encased in an upright coffin
Of milky iridescent ice. Entranced by a vision
Of green hills and pure blue skies without,
She conceives freedom and flight!
She must memorize the tune as the ice moves in
To touch her on every side and on her head.
As the last, haunting note is played
The child wakes up. Of course the tune is gone.
It is always gone.

This gothic episode, framed like the experience of sleep-paralysis, enacts an essential link between the bubbling-up of memory and the child's creative sources. In a deft segue to the penultimate verse, pace quickens with clipped phrasing and strong verbs, as the now eighteen-year-old child heads East by train. Her "layover in Minneapolis" is part of "a secret plan" she has "nurtured for ten years"; rushing with nickels to a pay phone, she looks up "Gerda Johnson" and is crushed to find "four columns, closely printed" of the same name.

Action shifts dramatically when "She calls from the top / As the hands of the clock spin round." Her cry now echoes the young child's "Gerda, don't leave!" in the third line of the poem:

Gerda! Gerda! Half-a-page
With answers none, or ancient whispery Norse voices
Down a tunnel of years, and oceans crossed
And cold home villages abandoned long ago.
Then she runs out of change and time. A train to catch.

As she has done only once—in the poem's opening line—the speaker again addresses Gerda directly as *"you,"* while the poem takes a surprise turn:

Gerda, you trudge down the walk forever;
The child, no matter how she calls and cries,
Cannot catch up.
Now from another life she summons you
Out of earth or aether, wherever you are,
Gerda, come back, to nurse your desolate child.

This final verse inevitably demonstrates the dynamic of a psyche under pressure. Heavy consonants, multiple caesuras, and the end-stop of line one all convey the deadening weight of repeating sorrow. Feelings of hopelessness and failure in lines two and three are accomplished with the help of slant rhyme, alliteration, onomatopoeia, and consonant clustering which lead to the spondaic, short-breathed "Cannot catch up." The marvelous half double-rhyme of "earth" and "aether" (and its associative rhyme with "life") suffuse the vatic pitch of lines four and five. And second-person voice does double-duty as it switches between Gerda and the speaker four times. Such complexity in six short lines. How easily our eye and nerve are guided through alternations of person and emphasis.

"Gerda," which began with a cry of abandonment, ends in a cry of exposure. Like a vessel that can never empty nor ever fill, the "child" closes the narrative circle: "the tune. . . is always gone." Here and elsewhere, Kizer's syntax controls simultaneity of revelation and event. "Gerda" shifts as it moves, and to paraphrase Roethke: it moves like the mind; it is imaginatively *right.*

Dislocations of time and space also work to enhance the narrative structure of "Twelve O'clock," a long autobiographical tour de force about atomic physics and physicists. At once engaging, witty, historical, the poem achieves a striking variety of tonal effects; and in this case, Kizer's poetics parallel scientific processes of thought. A great story, well-told, closes as the speaker (now in the Berkeley library) summons her seventeen-year-old self on that mid-century day (in the Princeton library) when Professor Einstein came out for lunch at noon: "The old man and the girl, smiling at one another." Central questions of existence—given new shape in our century—linger in the reader's mind. Relativity, randomness, fission, and the Heisenberg principle have all made appearances. But however expansive the theory, the mind must still frame it with specifics—visual, mathematical, verbal—to gaze ever more deeply into the cave. And it is Kizer's consummate 'verbal skill,' her coextensive marriage of micro and macro, that gives "Twelve O'Clock" such haunting power.

Poems in Kizer's previous five collections span a wide network of relations with family, friends, colleagues, lovers. Eight such poems in *Harping On* delightfully subvert expectation, as in the sonnet "Reunion:"

> For more than thirty years we hadn't met.
> I remembered the bright query of your face,
> That single-minded look, intense and stern,
> Yet most important—how could I forget?—
> Was what you taught me inadvertently
> (tutored by books and parents, even more
> By my own awe at what was yet to learn):
> The finest intellect can be a bore.
>
> At this, perhaps, our final interview,
> Still luminous with your passion to instruct,
> You speak to that recalcitrant pupil who
> Inhaled the chalk-dust of your rhetoric.
> I nod, I sip my wine, I praise your view,
> Grateful, my dear, that I escaped from you.

We are so slyly set up for the mordant surprise ending each verse. In another poem, entitled "An American Beauty," the history of a friendship—inflected with details of the 20th century roller coaster awaiting gifted women—is expressed in a tightly controlled lyric, at once heartbreaking and buoyant. It is addressed to her late friend who died from breast cancer, Ann London, the researcher and writer of the legislation for the Equal Rights Amendment. Another, "Arthur's Party," is a gas—a quirky tribute of encouragement and word play addressed to a childhood friend now an artist.

Also included are four translations: one by Li Po, two by Ingeborg Bachman, and a feisty "Tirade for the Next-to-Last Act" ("I'm leaving you, I won't touch you anymore.") by Nina Cassian, the Romanian poet, translator, and close friend of Paul Celan. There is an extra bonus with the Cassian poem: Kizer includes her own version (at the back of the book) in "Antique Hipster," a method she has devised "to avoid writing 'translatese' and to loosen up." It's a riot. Another riot is "In Hell with Virg and Dan," a Kizer original that *stayed* in Antique Hipster. Its memorable translation of the Usurers in CANTO XVII was probably raw enough that journal editors "quite properly rejected [it] for irreverence and 'not fitting in" (from an endnote).

In a review of Denise Levertov's *Light up the Cave* (New Directions, 1981), Kizer quotes Levertov: "The true heroes and heroines of political radicalism are those who maintain a rich inner life." Kizer herself adds ". . . a part of that rich life is a saving sense of humor, a delight in play, a self-directed irony, . . . and a life enriched by reading, myth, and dream." This blending is of course the very mix that sets Kizer's own poetry apart. And as she writes here, in "Fin-de-Siécle Blues," ". . . it's been one hell of a century." Her steady charting of its tyrannies, injustices, and absurdities, harp right alongside a compelling personal search to give order and unity to the chaotic impressions and desires of her individual spirit. If you agree that poets create culture, place yourself for a time in the hands of this writer whose deeply-textured stories demonstrate how the radical disjunctions of high modernism can blend with more traditional forms to create a uniquely contemporary voice.

Review by Hannah Stein

Millennial Qualms

No Moon. Eimers, Nancy. West Lafayette, IN: Purdue University Press. 1997.
84 pp. $12.95 paper.

Reading Nancy Eimers makes me think about the different kinds of worlds writ-
ers can create. And that leads me to think about different kinds of freedom we
define in those worlds: freedom as escape from capture or slavery; freedom to
choose among possibilities. It is generally writers in a foreign or disenfranchised
tradition who are forced to a reductive view of freedom—the sheer possession of
their own bodies. Such writers have a fervor—not to say zeal—about what
they know. The passion in their conviction and experience almost physically
appropriates the reader's own sensibility: I mean of course such writers as
Celan or Akhmatova who have had the misfortune to live in interesting times.

As do we all, in one way or another. It is a case of how we collide with the
time and place in which we do live. Nancy Eimers in her new book, *No Moon,*
employs her freedom to give thoughtful voice to ambivalence, to hesitation and
contrariety. When, in cracking the surface of appearance, a poet such as Eimers
shows the demons that lurk for her below that surface, she gives sanction to our
own tremors and hesitations regarding the world in which we find ourselves.
Her willingness to follow those demons into haunted, contrary, elusive terri-
tory gives her adroit poetry its power and allure.

Eimers's interesting time and place consist of a present-day urban suburbia
on the one hand and, on the other, an abiding nature. These are her here and
now: the dark chill of Michigan's winters versus the brief optimism of its sum-
mer; the city's vapid material life opposed by a skeptical and redemptive
imagination.

Nancy Eimers admits us into her world from the start. The first poem,
"Outer Space," clues us to the integrity within which she functions: her uncom-
promising refusal to harbor any notion she can't believe in. Exploring intima-
tions of directionlessness, the poet faces without flinching the perilous other
side of the known. She beguiles a reader to range and ponder with her through
a zone of questions without answers, keeping faith with the admission she
makes at the outset:

I don't remember an answering
just the vertigo of ascent, just the looking over a cliff
that is any question. . .
a lifting up of a human voice
that could not lie and could not promise to lift us
out of disrepair

Within Eimers' vertiginous emotional landscape of no promises, no lies, no uplift, she lets us let her guide us.

Her question in "Live Oaks," "What did we curse with our thanks everlasting?" opens up a Pandora's box. The fluid past, *that which has happened and is history*, can't be even falsely pinned down by memory's equivocations, because, as in "Wind," it "wears us down/ in a time too big for us to know." In the remarkable "Lakes" her father's gardening glove becomes the needle's eye through which Eimers may enter the heaven of an idealized childhood. She poses:

inside that glove
all motion stops, or *did it blow away*
on a wind that glances off the water
and sways a neighbor's dock
so rowboats clang together
like a row of dusty bells?   (italics added)

The transitory, the fluid, the not-quite suffuse her writing with total uncertainty or at best the certainty of change. She employs various modes of encoding change: "Anything/ could shake that house apart. . ." "*This little light of mine. . .//* guttered out in my fingers. . ." "And as the night brings blackness leaf by leaf/ she lights the wick of every blessed oak/ then lets them burn as one great tree." The past bears witness in "Lakes" against the present:

And if the single garden glove
could tug at the Chinese elm
and earth and sky begin to tip,
wouldn't the tree give way
with all its crumbly roots
and fall into the sky?

Eimers' elegiac note both ennobles the past and suggests the futility of expecting it to redeem the present.

190

"Autistic Twins at the Fireworks" asks brilliantly in the children's voice, but asks for us all, "What are we doing here?/ Autistics. Half-wits. Morons. Angels. Idiot savants.// Words, like the vanishings you have come out to celebrate." What Eimers continually celebrates is that we are able to endure a constant instability in the ambiguous relation of Self to World. The magic and subtlety of her language act out that instability; she conjoins the earthy imagery of "the stink of your cherry bombs, your ash-worms toiling out of pellets" with a line like "you see each burst of sparks in its instant, unmediated."

The other side of a principled refusal to accept easy answers is to long for them. These poems' desire for an unattainable security shows up in Eimers' obsession with shelter as icon, exposure as ache. There is much sadness, much discomfort in the moods of "The common nighthawk lays its eggs on a gravel roof,/ no nest—" and "already I have lain awake/ as wind howls out the shape of the house." *Tous conforts* is what she wants, yet *tous conforts* is never what she gets: "To live inside was the simple first idea behind a house:// a noun// but soft inside. Lined by down" ("Unplugged"); "thanks for tucking us in like silverware folded in linen napkins" ("Live Oaks").

But . . . "I could FEEL the buildings shaken down to their girders" ("The Match Girl"); "In Kalamazoo it is snowing eternally/ Like notes on the rolls of a player piano" ("In the New Year"); and "Poor little girl. She has no home./ / She has no voice/ but the pines" ("Unplugged"). No false solace here.

Many of the poems are strewn with bars, bowling alleys, pizza joints, each with its emblem, its noise, its neon effulgence. All these, and more, incite toward sleeplessness, one of Eimers' designated betes-noires. Her intimate encounters with diners and parking lots and penny arcades, the grit and fiz of working-class efforts to survive, could be seen as a balancing act—balancing against the inventiveness, both wild and subtle, of her writing. Except that it's not an act at all; the rootedness in bland working-class suburbia seems completely genuine. This poet knows whereof she speaks; the very grime has authenticity. But there's no prettification, no seductiveness:

"Not a question that drives you out of Self
like a moth to its porch-light epipsychidion
but a question that drives you into Self
like the soul of a rock in torrential rains." ("Outer Space)

Not often does Eimers use abstruse words; when she does they knock you out.

Eimers ranges far for her craft. A simile can be so inevitable that we wonder why we never thought before, say, of this rendering of Niagara: "The frozen falls looks like a stand of trees." But such a figure's closure is countered more often than not by the haunting, elusive unfolding of lines such as "To look at the moon is to open up little bottles and boxes,// beach glass, blue jay feathers, clearies, cat's-eyes,/ heart of a hummingbird, snowdrift, fingernails, rain." This kind of writing presupposes the kind of alert, demanding, visionary reader who reads poetry to delight the ear and to learn.

There's formal diversity in this poetry; within the pliant rubric of free verse Eimers allows herself long lines and short, strophe and irregularity. "Like me," she says, "(mother) thinks in metaphor: if she slipped/ out of focus, she might be a marsh,// treeless, periodically inundated." But anytime this poet seems to be formally slipping from focus, careful attention shows that her meanings travel purposefully through the images, as in "Absent Bird Moon."

In this, one of the most captivating of the poems, her keenly wrought questions can be slightly disingenuous. A reader is not surprised to find that questions fill the poem, both explicit: "Moon, why can't you see how meaning drifts to its leaf, as I see/ the Pizza Hut on the corner is a ruby awake all night?" and implicit: "I don't know what to call this"—to which her temporizing answer is:

Nothing, born each second and hung by its thread,
so what do we do if the moons escape,
do we drown in the ocean of yellow leaves?
Would it give us something to talk about?

Taking Eimers' cue, to continue in questioning mode: are these questions rhetorical, or are we being let into the secret of a deep despondency? The fine balance the poet maintains between affirmation and annulment keeps the reader on edge. In "A Night Without Stars" she speaks to millennial qualms with a kind of macabre and Prufrockian wit:

"And the lake was a dark spot
                    on a lung.
Some part of its peace was dead; the rest was temporary."

The friction of uncertainty endows Eimers' poetry with tension and unease. Her forms and language partly resolve that tension with an authority that commands trust. Nancy Eimers has investigated the discomforts of the soul in ways from which we can safely learn and be exhilarated. Poetry, after all, while engaging us in a kind of temporary transformation into the Other, ultimately restores us more insightfully to ourselves.

It shouldn't come as a surprise when an ordinary kind of place—suburbia—is found giving life to so much memory and metaphor, to such trembling expectation: the hope of nothing worse to come. What Nancy Eimers has to say to us hovers very close to concerns of the end of the century. The old saying rings true: there's nothing that is not political. Try to squirm out of that assertion as we may, at bottom there is zeal and there is absence of zeal. Zeal means trouble. Its absence permits us to live with opposites. Through negative capability—the tolerance for opposites—we no longer need to define ourselves by what we are not: those unequivocal out side lines that may be drawn around the self. Instead, what feels its way freely from inside becomes the shape we cannot know until our faltering attempts, our mistakes and misapprehensions—our living—call it forth from us.

This highly crafted poetry is a pleasure to read. Apart from poems already cited, some of those I liked best are "A History of Navigation," "The Match Girl," "The Pelican Girl," and "No Moon." The ironies Eimers employs to grapple with her obsessions—birds, moons, city streets, her very misgivings—become more lyric than we have any right to expect irony to be. Of course far more than craft is afoot here. In this poetry that a reader can confront spiritually and head on, Nancy Eimers challenges the ordinary: what are we to make of our lives?

Contributors

Marjorie Agosín was born in Maryland, and raised in Chile. A poet and Human Rights activist, she has authored several collections of poetry, literary criticism and a memoir about her mother growing up as a Jewish girl in Chile. She is a Professor of Spanish at Wellesley College.

Renée Ashley won the Brittingham Prize in Poetry for her first collection *Salt*. Her most recent book is *The Various Reasons of Light*. She is Assistant Poetry Coordinator for the Geraldine R. Dodge Foundation.

John Balaban has twice been nominated for the National Book Award. His most recent book is *Spring Essence: The Poetry of Ho Xuan Huong* (Copper Canyon Press).

Dorothy Barresi is the author of *All of the Above*, winner of the 1990 Barnard New Women Poet's Prize and *The Post-Rapture Diner* (University of Pittsburgh Press). She is an Associate Professor of English at California State University, Northridge, where she teaches creative writing and literature.

Ronald H. Bayes is the happy genius of poetry in Laurinburg, North Carolina. He is the founder of the *St. Andrews Review* and is the author of several collections of poetry including, *FRAM*, and *The Casket*. In 1999 a chair was endowed at St. Andrews College in Laurinburg in his honor.

Robin Becker won the 1996 Lambda Literary Award in Lesbian Poetry for her fourth collection, *All-American Girl*. Her most recent book is *The Horse Fair* (University of Pittsburgh Press). She is Associate Professor of English and Women's Studies at Pennsylvania State University.

John Bensko is a professor of English at the University of Memphis, is the author of three poetry collections: *Green Soldiers*, winner of the Yale Series of Younger Poets Award, *The Waterman's Children* and most recently, *The Iron City* (University of Illinois Press).

Al Benthall is a Ph.D. candidate in literature at UNC-Chapel Hill. He is a former poetry editor for the *Carolina Quarterly*.

Elyse Blankley is Professor of English and Chair of Women's Studies Department at California State University-Long Beach. Her reviews, critiques and essays have been published widely.

Laurel Ann Bogen is the author of eight volumes of poetry including *The Burning: New & Selected Poems, 1970-1990, The Last Girl in the Land of the Butterflies* and *Fission* (Red Dancefloor Press). She is an instructor of poetry and performance, and curates the Writers in Focus series at the Los Angeles County Museum of Art.

Andrea Hollander Budy is Writer-in-Residence at Lyon College. She is the author of three chapbooks and two full-length collections of poems, including *The Other Life* (Story Line Press) and *House Without a Dreamer* (Story Line Press), which won the Nicholas Roerich Poetry Prize.

Michael Burns has published poetry in numerous journals, including *Kenyon Review, Poetry, Southern Review,* and *Missouri Review.* Professor of English at Southwest Missouri State University in Springfield, Burns is editor of *Miller Williams and the Poetry of the Particular.* He is the author of *The Secret Names* (University of Missouri Press).

Kay Stripling Byer is the author of three collections of poetry, among them, *Wildwood Flower,* the 1992 Lamont Poetry Selection of the Academy of American Poets and most recently *Black Shawl.* She lives in Western North Carolina.

Jari Chevalier is a poet, fiction writer and teacher. She was recently a member of the Adjunct Faculty of Antioch University in Santa Barbara and is a Contributing Editor to the poetry journal *Barrow Street.* Widely published, she is the creator of a respected and unique program of creative writing workshops for authors.

Lucille Clifton is the author of ten books of poetry including *The Terrible Stories* and *Blessing the Boats: New & Selected Poems 1988-2000* (both from BOA Editions). She is Distinguished Professor of Humanities at St. Mary's College of Maryland, and she is a Chancellor of The Academy of American Poets.

Jeanette Marie Clough is the author of a chapbook, *Dividing Paradise,* and a full-length collection, *Celestial Burn: New and Selected Poems* (Sacred Beverage Press). She works at the Getty Research Institute in Los Angeles.

Martha Collins' work has been featured in *American Poetry Review.* She is the author of *A History of Small Life On A Windy Planet* (University of Georgia Press), *The Arrangement of Space* (Peregrine Smith).

T. Crunk was born and raised in western Kentucky. He has received master's degrees in philosophy from the University of Kentucky and in English and creative writing from the University of Virginia. His book, *Living in the Resurrection,* was chosen by James Dickey for the Yale Series of Younger Poets Award.

Kate Daniels is the author of three books of poetry, most recently, *Four Testimonies*, and teaches poetry in the English Department at Vanderbilt University. She was the director of the recently held Millennial Gathering of the Writers of the New South, the most significant gathering of Southern writers in more than 65 years.

Christopher Davis is an associate professor of creative writing at the University of North Carolina at Charlotte. He is the author of *The Tyrant of the Past and the Slave of the Future*, past winner of the Associated Writing Programs Award for Poetry. His most recent collection is *The Patriot* (University of Georgia Press)

Glover Davis has published three books, *Bandaging Bread*, *August Fires*, and *Legend* (Wesleyan University Press). He is the Director of the M.F.A. program at San Diego State University.

Mark Doty has published five volumes of poetry and two memoirs. He is a winner of Britain's T. S. Eliot Prize, and he has also won a Whiting Writer's Award, the National Book Critics Circle Award, and the *Los Angeles Times* Book Award.

Sharon Doubiago is a poet, essayist, and short story writer. Her books of poetry include *Hard Country*, *South America Mi Hija*, *Psyche Drives the Coast* and *The Husband Arcane*. *The Arcane of O*. Her most recent book is *Body and Soul* (Cedar Hill Publications).

Joseph Duemer has written two books of poetry, *Customs* and *Static*. With Jim Simmerman, he coedited the anthology *Dog Music*.

Denise Duhamel is the author of ten books and chapbooks of poetry. *The Star-Spangled Banner* was a recent winner of the Crab Orchard Poetry Prize from Southern Illinois University Press. She has been anthologized widely, including three volumes of *The Best American Poetry* series.

Terry Ehret's first book, *Lost Body* was selected by Carolyn Kizer for the National Poetry Series. She teaches English at Santa Rosa Junior College and lives in Petaluma, California with her husband and three daughters.

Donald Finkel is the distinguished author of fourteen books, two have been nominated for the National book Critics' Circle Award, another was finalist for the National Book Award. A Guggenheim Fellow, he taught for forty-one years at Washington University in St. Louis and has served as a visiting professor at Bennington College and Princeton Universtiy. He is now retired and lives in St. Louis. His most recent collection is *A Question of Seeing* (University of Arkansas Press).

Michael C Ford is a poet and writer from Los Angeles who made his poetic debut at a reading with Jim Morrison of the Doors. He is the author of more than 20 books of poetry including his newest *Emergency Exits: The Selected Poems 1970-1995* (Amaranth Editions).

Dana Gioia is a poet, critic, editor, and translator who has published two poetry collections, *Daily Horoscope* and *The Gods of Winter*. He has written extensively on Weldon Kees, and collected some of Kees' prose into the book *The Ceremony and Other Stories*.

Jeanne Girolo-Hoffman lives and writes in rural San Luis Obispo and Sonoma counties in California, and in Europe.

Patricia Goedicke has published eleven volumes of poetry, including: *Invisible Horses* and *The Tongues We Speak: New and Selected Poems*, named one of the best books of the year by *The New York Times Book Review*. Her newest collection is *As Earth Begins to End*, from Copper Canyon. She teaches Creative Writing at the University of Montana, and was married for thirty years to the late Leonard Wallace Robinson, a *New Yorker* writer, poet, and widely published author of short stories and novels.

Jeffrey Greene lives in Paris. His poetry has appeared in *The New Yorker, Ploughshares, Parnassus,* and *Poetry.* He has three books of poetry; *American Spirituals* (Northeastern University Press), *Glimpses of the Invisible World in New Haven* (Coreopsis Books) and *To the Left of the Worshiper* (alicejamesbooks).

C. G. Hanzlicek is Professor of English and Director of Creative Writing at California State University, Fresno. He is the author of eight collections of poetry, the most recent of which is forthcoming from the University of Pittsburgh Press, *The Cave: Selected and New Poems.*

Colette Inez has authored several collections of poetry including, *The Woman Who Loved Worms, Alive and Taking Names, Eight Minutes from the Sun,* and *Family Life.* The most recent collection, *Clemency* was published by Carnegie Mellon University Press.

Benjamin Ivry is the author of *Paradise for the Portuguese Queen* (Orchises Press). He lives in New York City.

Gray Jacobik is the author of *The Double Task* (University of Massachusetts Press), winner of the Juniper Prize, and *The Surface of Last Scattering* (Texas Review Press), winner of the X.J. Kennedy Poetry Prize. She also has appeared in *The Best American Poetry* series.

200

Mark Jarman's collection of poetry, *Questions for Ecclesiastes*, won the Lenore Marshall Poetry Prize for 1998 and was a finalist for the 1997 National Book Critics Circle Award. He is the co-editor of *Rebel Angels: 25 Poets of the New Formalism*, and co-author of *The Reaper Essays*. His book of essays, *The Secret of Poetry*, and his new collection of poetry, *Unholy Sonnets*, are from Story Line Press. He teaches at Vanderbilt University.

Donald Justice is one of the most distinguished poets in the United States. Among his many honors and awards is the Pulitzer Prize for his *Selected Poems*. His recent books include *A Donald Justice Reader* and *New and Selected Poems* (Alfred A. Knopf). He is a Chancellor of The Academy of American Poets.

Weldon Kees was a painter, critic, and one of the most respected American poets of the 20th century. His disappearance in 1955 is presumed a suicide.

Carolyn Kizer received the Pulitzer Prize for *YIN* in 1985. Her most recent collection, *Cool, Calm & Collected: Poems, 1961–2000* is from Copper Canyon. Her groundbreaking long poem, *Pro Femina*, published in three parts over a period of thirty five years is collected into a chapbook from University of Missouri - Kansas City Press. With husband, architect John Woodbridge, she divides her time between homes in Northern California and Paris.

Ron Koertge is a widely published poet and Young Adult author, and a professor of English at Pasadena City College, Pasadena, California. He has published many books of poetry including *Making Love to Roget's Wife - Poems New and Selected* (University of Arkansas Press). He has also appeared in *The Best American Poetry* series.

Ted Kooser lives in Garland, Nebraska. A new book of poems written during his 1998-1999 recovery from cancer surgery and radiation, *Winter Morning Walks: 100 Postcards to Jim Harrison* is forthcoming from Carnegie Mellon University Press.

Paul Lawson lives in Washington, DC where he operates The Charioteer Press. His poems have appeared in *Poetry, The New Yorker,* and many other journals.

Richard Levine teaches school in New York City. His work has appeared in numerous literary journals including the premier issue of *Rattapallax*.

Alexander Long lives in Silver Spring, Maryland. With Christopher Buckley, he is editing *A Condition of the Spirit*, a book on the life and work of Larry Levis, for the University of Georgia Press. His work has appeared in *The Cream City Review, Connecticut Review, Montserrat Review* and elsewhere.

Adrian C. Louis teaches at Southwest State University in Marshall, Minnesota. His most recent book of poems is *Ancient Acid Flashes Back* (University of Nevada Press).

Suzanne Lummis is the author of *In Danger* (Roundhouse Press) a recent selection in the California Poetry Series. Her other books include *Idiosyncracies* and *Falling Short of Heaven*. She is the founding director of the Los Angeles Poetry Festival and an editor of *Grand Passion: The Poetry of Los Angeles and Beyond*.

Sarah Maclay is the author of *Weeding the Duchess* (Black Stone Press) and *Fugue States Coming Down the Hall*, a piece for the stage anthologized in *Scenarios: Scripts to Perform* (Assembling Press). Her poetry has appeared in *Blue Satellite, Spillway, Deadstart, The Borrowed Times, 51%* and *The Squaw Valley Review*. She currently lives in Venice, California.

Nancy Mairs is the author of two collections of poetry, *And Now It Is Winter* and *All the Rooms of the Yellow House* which received the Western States' Book Award for Poetry. She is greatly admired for her brilliant essay collections: *Plaintext, Carnal Acts, Ordinary Time*, and *Waist High in the World*. She lives in Tucson, Arizona.

Dionisio D. Martínez, born in Cuba, is the author of *Climbing Back* (Norton), selected by Jorie Graham for the National Poetry Series. His other books include, *Bad Alchemy* (Norton) and *History as a Second Language*.

Valarie Martínez is the author of *Absence, Luminescent* (Four Way Books). Her work has appeared in *The Best American Poetry* series, *The Bread Loaf Anthology of New American Poets* (University of New England Press) and *American Poetry: Next Generation* (Carnegie Mellon).

J. D. McClatchy is the author of four books of poetry, most recently, *Ten Commandments* (Alfred A. Knopf). He is also an essayist and has written four opera libretti. He is the editor of *The Yale Review*, and a Chancellor of The Academy of American Poets.

Robert McDowell with his wife, Lysa McDowell is the publisher of the very fine small press, Story Line Press in Ashland, Oregon. He is the author of two collections of poetry, *Quiet Money* and *The Diviners*.

Elnora McNaughton is the author of two books of poetry, *After the Garden* and *Hold the Moon Bursting* (Mille Grazie Press). Her poems have been published widely. She makes her home in Oxnard, California where she also nurtures a love for Traditional Jazz.

Errol Miller lives in Monroe, Louisiana and has recently published poems in *Blue Satellite, American Poetry Review, The Bitter Oleander* and other literary journals.

Peter Money is the author of five books of poetry including *These Are My Shoes* (Boz Publishing), and most recently *Finding It: Selected Poems* (Mille Grazie Press). He lives in Berkeley, California.

Elizabeth Seydel Morgan is the author of three collections of poetry, *Parties, The Governor of Desire*, most recently, *On Long Mountain*.

David Mura is the author of two collections of poetry, *After We Lost Our Way*, a winner of the National Poetry Series Award, and *The Colors of Desire* (Anchor/Doubleday).

Jim Natal is the author of *Oil on Paper* (The Inevitable Press) and *Explaining Water With Water* (The Inevitable Press). His first full-length collection, *In the Bee Trees*, is published by Archer Books.

Harry E. Northup has published six books of poems, most recently, *The Ragged Vertical* (Cahuenga Press). He is also an actor, appearing in more than thirty-four feature films.

William Olsen is the author of *The Hand of God and a Few Bright Flowers*, a winner of the National Poetry Series competition, and *Vision of a Storm Cloud* (TriQuarterly Press). He teaches at Western Michigan University.

Mary Elizabeth Perez is a native of Tampa, Florida. She was awarded the Hillsborough County Emerging Artist Grant for Poetry. Her work has appeared in *Borderlands, Texas Poetry Review, The Christian Science Monitor*. An essay by Dionisio Martínez featuring several of her poems has appeared in the Academy of American Poets Quarterly, *The American Poet*.

David Pink is a poet and writer who teaches at Moorehead State University in Minnesota. He has published poetry, fiction, and essays in the *North Atlantic Review, Prairie Schooner, Salmagundi, South Dakota Review, Western Humanities Review*, and *North Coast Review*.

Holly Prado is a poet, writer, reviewer and teacher. Her most recent book is *Esperanza: Poems for Orpheus* (Cahuenga Press). Her other books include *Nothing Breaks Off at the Edge, Losses*, and *Specific Mysteries*. She teaches creative writing both privately and in the graduate program of the University of Southern California.

Margaret Rabb is the author of *Granite Dives* (New Issues Press). She lives in Chapel Hill, North Carolina with her husband and twin daughters.

Carlos Reyes lives in Portland, Oregon. He is the author of several collections of poetry, among them *A Suitcase Full of Crows*, *Nightmarks* and *Men of Our Time: Anthology*. His work has been published in numerous journals and magazines.

David Rigsbee co-edited *Invited Guest: Southern Poetry in the Twentieth Century*, an anthology forthcoming from The University Press of Virginia. His most recent collection of poetry is *A Skeptic's Notebook: Longer Poems* (St. Andrews Press). He is the author of *Styles of Ruin: Joseph Brodsky and the Postmodernist Elegy* (Greenwood Press) and *Trailers* (Virginia). He lives with his family in Raleigh, North Carolina. His wife is the painter, Jill Bullitt.

Alberto Ríos is Regents Professor of English at Arizona State University. His books of poetry include *Teodora Luna's Two Kisses*, *The Lime Orchard Woman*, *Five Indiscretions* and *Whispering to Fool the Wind*, which won the Academy of American Poets' Walt Whitman Award.

Kay Ryan is the author of five collections of poetry, including *Elephant Rocks*. Her work has been published in *The New Yorker*, *The American Poetry Review*, and other journals. Her newest collection, is *Say Uncle*, from Grove/Alantic.

Dennis Saleh is the author of five books of poetry. His most recent book is *Rhymses' Book* (Quicksilver). *This Is Not Surrealism* was winner of the first chapbook competition from Willamette River Books. He is also the publisher of Comma Books.

Sherod Santos is a poet and essayist. He is the author of four books of poetry, *Accidental Weather*, *The Southern Reaches*, *The City of Women* and, most recently, *The Pilot Star Elegies* (W. W. Norton). He is professor of English at the University of Missouri - Columbia.

Charlie Smith is the author of five collections of poems and five novels. His most recent book is *Heroin: And Other Poems* (W.W. Norton). His other books include *The Palms* and *Before and After*, both also released by Norton. He lives in New York City.

Hannah Stein lives in Davis, California. Her book, *Earthlight*, is the first volume in the La Questa Press Poetry Series. Her chapbook, *Schools of Flying Fish*, was published by State Street Press. She is an editor of *Americas Review*.

Pamela Stewart received her M.F.A. from the University of Iowa and after teaching for several years, a Guggenheim Fellowship took her to Cornwall, U.K. where she lived for seven years. She is the author of *Infrequent Mysteries* (alicejamesbooks) and *The Red Suitcase*. She lives in western Massachusetts.

Alberta T. Turner is the author of *Beginning with And: New and Selected Poems* (Bottom Dog Press). Her other books include *Learning to Count, Lid and Spoon,* and *A Belfry of Knees.* She is Professor Emerita at Cleveland State University where she directed the CSU Poetry Center and Poetry Series.

Belle Waring has written two books of poetry, *Refuge,* winner of the Associated Writing Programs' Award for Poetry, and *Dark Blonde* (Sarabande Books) winner of the first annual Levis Reading Prize from Virginia Commonwealth University. She teaches creative writing at Children's Hospital in Washington, DC.

Florence Weinberger is the author of two books of poetry, *The Invisible Telling Its Shape* (Fithian Press) and *Breathing Like a Jew* (Blue Chickory Press). She lives in Encino, California.

Bruce Williams has published two poetry chapbooks, *Holistic Dressing* (Pudding House) and *Stratification* (The Inevitable Press). He is Professor of English at Mt. San Antonio College in Walnut, California, near Los Angeles, where he has been teaching an on-line creative writing course for the past three years.

Terence Winch is the author of *Irish Musicians/American Friends,* which won an American Book Award, *Contenders,* a collection of short stories, and most recently *The Great Indoors: Poems* (Story Line Press). Winch has also recorded three albums with Celtic Thunder, one of the leading traditional Irish bands in the US. He lives in the Washington, DC area.

Baron Wormser is the author of five collections of poetry, most recently *When* (Sarabande Books) and *Mulroney & Others* (Sarabande Books). He lives with his wife in Hallowell, Maine.

Robert Wynne has written two poetry chapbooks: *Driving* (The Inevitable Press) and *Patterns of Breathing* (Mille Grazie Press). He received his MFA from Anitoch University in Los Angeles. Twice a winner of the Academy of American Poets Award, he now lives in Fort Worth, Texas.